Joel Comiskey

MW01616346

how to
lead a GREAT
small group.
meeting

{ so people want to come back }

CCS PUBLISHING.
Moreno Valley, California U.S.A.

Praise for

how to lead a GREAT
small group meeting

"Comiskey has hit one out of the park! This book will not collect dust on my bookshelf! I'll use it over and over again as a reference tool in the groups I lead and oversee. And I plan to have every one of my group leaders read it as well."
MIKE MACK
Founder, smallgroups.com
Small Groups Pastor, Northeast Christian Church

"Only when the Holy Spirit touches a person's heart in the safe environment of a well planned small group meeting do we truly see the incredible plan in which God has invited us to participate. In *How To Lead A Great Small Group Meeting*, Joel has captured the essence of leading life-changing small group meetings and given us a practical road map to success!"
THOM CORRIGAN
Pastor, Founder - Pilgrimage Training
Author of Experiencing Community

"Wow! This book taught this old dog a few new tricks. I read this book and immediately made two changes in my facilitation style.
Joel, thanks for the tips!"
RANDALL NEIGHBOUR
Senior Editor, CellGroup Journal

"If you've ever led a small group meeting, you'll find yourself nodding in agreement with Comiskey's honest struggles and helpful advice. Without being overly simplistic, Joel synthesizes the many parts of leading a small group meeting. As a small group leader and trainer I've waited a long time for a tool like this."
TOM BRUNNER
Senior Pastor, Hope Church

"Joel Comiskey is one of the world's leading authorities on the subject of small group ministry. Because he writes from an experiential rather than theoretical perspective, he offers valuable insights that can transform your small group ministry into a *great* ministry. This book is required reading for every group leader and pastor who desires to lead an effective ministry in their church."
TERRY CANTRELL
Sr. Pastor, Wesleyan Fellowship

how to lead a
GREAT
small group meeting

. . . so people want to come back

JOEL COMISKEY

CCS PUBLISHING.
Moreno Valley, California U.S.A.

Published by CCS Publishing
Moreno Valley, CA 92557
888-511-9995 • www.joelcomiskeygroup.com

Cover design by Neubauer Design Group
Interior Illustrations by Don Bleyl
Text design by Rick Chandler
Editing by Scott Boren

ISBN# 978-1-950069-11-8

CCS Publishing primarily publishes materials that resource the
worldwide cell church movement.

Find us on the World Wide Web at
https://www.joelcomiskeygroup.com

Acknowledgments

I owe a debt of gratitude to those who have made this book possible:

- ➤ Scott Boren, editor
- ➤ Rick Chandler, publishing production/graphic design
- ➤ Don Bleyl, illustrator

This team added to the book's personality, taking it from the manuscript stage to book form.

Special thanks to Michael Mack, a prolific small group author and founder of smallgroups.com, for providing key insight.

Two resources have been especially helpful in writing this book: *Cell Group Journal* and *smallgroups.com,* an online ministry dedicated to equipping small group leaders. In this book, I've drawn heavily from both of them, and I highly recommend them.

I especially want to thank my wife and children for their encouragement to me throughout the writing of this book.

Contents

Introduction

Silence. Jerry's attempt to stimulate discussion failed. "Is there anyone else who'd like to comment on this verse?" Still no response. Jerry decided it was best to break the silence by launching into a spontaneous comment about a few Bible passages. "At least they're receiving God's Word," he assured himself.

I know how this leader felt. I've faced similar periods of strained silence as I led the lessons in my own small group. More than once I've thought to myself, "Why are my own discussion times so dry? What's the missing link?"

Many small group leaders, immersed in the battle, doubt their talent and leadership skills. They blame their personality or an apparent lack of gifting for the barren lessons, the uneasiness in the group, and the fact that only a few people participate.

The good news is that the vast majority of small group problems are solvable. I've written this book to help you turn a dry gathering into a dynamic meeting.

Small Group Interest

Seventy-five million adult Americans regularly attend a small group (not including all the teenagers and children in groups). There are 300,000 churches in the U.S., but more than three million small groups.[1]

With the interest in small groups growing, especially in the face of an impersonal internet society, the need is great to understand the dynamics of small groups (both to participate in as well as to lead). Lyle Schaller, after listing 20 innovations in the modern U.S. church, says, "The decision by tens of millions of teenagers and adults to place a high personal priority on weekly participation in serious, in-depth, lay-led, and continuing Bible study and prayer groups is perhaps the most important of all."[2]

The small group phenomenon is certainly not limited to the U.S. The largest church in the history of Christianity, Yoido Full Gospel Church in Seoul, South Korea, is based on 25,000 small groups. The largest churches in the world, following the example of YFGC, are also based on small groups.[3]

Most secular organizations now hold regular small group meetings, from boards to task forces. Knowing how to lead such meetings not only sweetens the atmosphere, but it often determines business success or failure.

In fact, small group dynamics is a science in its own right. One of my first college courses covered it as we worked through the book *Effective Group Discussion*. We learned how to actively listen, respond positively, summarize, and many other small group skills.[4]

While secular organizations seek to increase productivity through small group dynamics, God's purposes must guide the Christian small group. Effective small group leaders live under the power of the Holy Spirit and communicate God's purposes for the group. The Christian leader will become more effective and more fully meet the needs of group members by learning the skills of small group dynamics.

Definition of a Small Group

Some experts choose the broad path and define "small group" as anything small that meets as a group. This definition is so inclusive (and elusive) that it doesn't clarify anything. The communists as well as liberation theologians promote their brand of small groups. Across the land, various types of groups are forming to heal physical disorders, chemical dependency, marital problems . . . and the list continues. With this broad definition, you could include a family, a classroom, church board meeting, a basketball team, and a Christian small group. Defining a small group by its size doesn't clarify the purpose of the group.

I define a small group as a *group of 3 to 15 people who meet weekly outside the church building for the purpose of evangelism, community, and spiritual growth with the goal of making disciples who make disciples that results in multiplication.*

I realize that many small groups are not connected to the local church. If you're leading such a group, this book will help you fine-tune your skills. But our focus is on church-based small groups.

When defining a small group, it's important to identify essential components or characteristics that should be present. Life-changing small groups should have the following characteristics:

➤ Upward Focus: Knowing God
➤ Inward Focus: Knowing each other
➤ Outward Focus: Reaching out to those who don't know Jesus (with the goal of multiplying the small group)
➤ Forward Focus: Raising up new leaders

Small groups should be consistent, yet flexible. Some groups, for example, might be more "seeker-sensitive" than others. Excessive singing and prayer wouldn't be appropriate in such meetings. Our church has many groups that meet on university campuses. The leaders purposely try to maintain a flavor that's appropriate in that context, since the main thrust is evangelism. Yet, even in these groups, the components of knowing God and relationship-building are present.

No two small groups are exactly alike, but each group maintains the same components: seeking God (upward focus); developing relationships with one another (inward focus); reaching out to non-Christians (outward focus); and developing new leaders (forward focus). These components allow small groups the flexibility to be effective, while at the same time achieving their goal.

Keep the Group Small

Bigger is not better for small groups. Growth in size excludes growth in intimacy.[5] Unless small groups remain small, they lose their effectiveness and ability to care for the needs of each member. When two people are in conversation, there are two communication lines; that number increases to 12 when four are present. With ten people, the number grows to 90, and when 15 people gather, there are 210 lines of communication. After 15 persons, there is no longer an opportunity for people to know each other intimately. It's a congregation, not a small group.

But how big is too big? One small group-driven church discovered ten was the maximum size.[7] Carl George agrees, emphatically declaring that ten is ". . . the time-tested, scientifically validated size that allows for optimal communication."[8]

John Mallison, however, finds room for a few more. He says, "Twelve not only sets the upper limit for meaningful relationships, but provides a non-threatening situation for those who are new to small group

What a Small Group is Not[6]

Sometimes we understand something better when we realize what it is not. The following constitutes erroneous thinking about small groups:

➤ *Club Status*
  Although you might focus on a homogeneous group, remember that your small group must continue to grow and eventually multiply. Don't allow homogeneity to become an end in itself.

➤ *A Clique*
  Small groups are wonderful because they move people into deep community. At the same time, we must always include others in our community since Christ has given us a commission to make disciples.

➤ *An Organization*
  This is a deadly trap. A small group is a *living organism* rather than simply a nice way to organize the body of Christ. A healthy small group functions as a living part of Christ's body.

➤ *Static*
  Cells in the human body that don't multiply will die. One small group guru told me that "small groups are born to die." I disagree. I believe that small groups are born to multiply. Yet, if a group does not multiply, it will die, and for this reason, a small group must continually reproduce itself.

➤ *One Day a Week*
  The small group is far more than another weekly meeting. It's a family. During the week, the members should pastor one another, care for one another, and befriend each other. I've discovered that small group members often look for each other during the weekend service time and even sit together. In one small group-driven church that I visited, each group was encouraged to meet together after the Sunday morning service for fellowship, accountability, and to plan for the next week.

➤ *A Classroom*
  I visited one small group in which the leader assumed the role as the Bible answer man. The meeting centered around the Bible guru (the small group leader) who taught the unlearned (the rest of small group members). The small group leader, rather, is a facilitator/shepherd, who guides the lesson while stimulating others to share.

> ### Just a Bible Study
> Many equate small groups with neighborhood Bible studies. While the lesson time in small groups is based on God's Word, the focus is on the application of God's Word in a participatory atmosphere, rather than on someone teaching Biblical knowledge. Remember the exhortation of James 1:22, "Do not merely listen to the word, and so deceive yourselves."
>
> ### A Therapy Group
> The small group is not a psychoanalysis session. Healing occurs in the small group through listening, empathy, and prayer. I believe in counseling sessions — but not in the small group.
>
> ### A Band of Renegades
> Small groups in a small group-driven church participate in the local church. Those who attend the group must also attend the congregational gatherings (or at least are constantly encouraged to attend) and those who attend the large gathering attend the small group. I strongly discourage small group leaders from inviting people from other churches to attend their group. It's unethical to pastor sheep from another congregation. Our groups focus on non-Christians and people from our own congregation.
>
> ### Prayer Group
> While prayer plays an essential role in the group, it's not the only focus.
>
> ### Task Group or Ministry Group
> Nor is a small group simply a task or ministry group (e.g., church board, ushers meeting before the service, etc). In such small groups, it's very hard, if not impossible for evangelism to take place — unless of course your church allows non-Christians to join the church board!

experiences . . . It is significant that Jesus chose twelve men to be in his group."[9] Striking a balance, Dale Galloway says, "The ideal number for good group dynamics and for caring and dialogue is somewhere between eight and twelve. Participation is much greater when you stay within those numbers."[10]

Galloway's advice not only sounds reasonable, but it also rings true with my own experience. Certainly a group should not grow beyond fifteen

Lines of Communication

N X N – N =
Communication Lines

$2 \times 2 - 2 = 2$
$4 \times 4 - 4 = 12$
$15 \times 15 - 15 = 210$

people, nor have fewer than five (with the possible exception of newly planted groups).

Visualizing the Small Group Meeting

The pictures throughout this book will help you visualize the skills you need to lead a great small group meeting. In order for your physical body to work properly, all of the individual parts must work together. The same is true of the small group meeting. Some small group leaders have great eyes, but have no soul. Others are all mouth, with no ears. But when all the parts are working, the meeting will flow. Each chapter in this book corresponds to a different body part.

➤ Chapter One - A Pure Heart: Prepare Yourself

➤ Chapter Two - Gathering Arms: How to Structure a Meeting

➤ Chapter Three - Legs that Support: Facilitating Others

➤ Chapter Four - An Open Soul: Practicing Transparency

➤ Chapter Five - An Inquisitive Mind: Asking Stimulating Questions

➤ Chapter Six - Listening Ears

➤ Chapter Seven - An Encouraging Tongue

➤ Chapter Eight - Warm Hands: Reaching Out to Non-Christians

➤ Chapter Nine - Walking Together: Moving Through the Stages of Life

➤ Chapter Ten - Eyes That See the Details

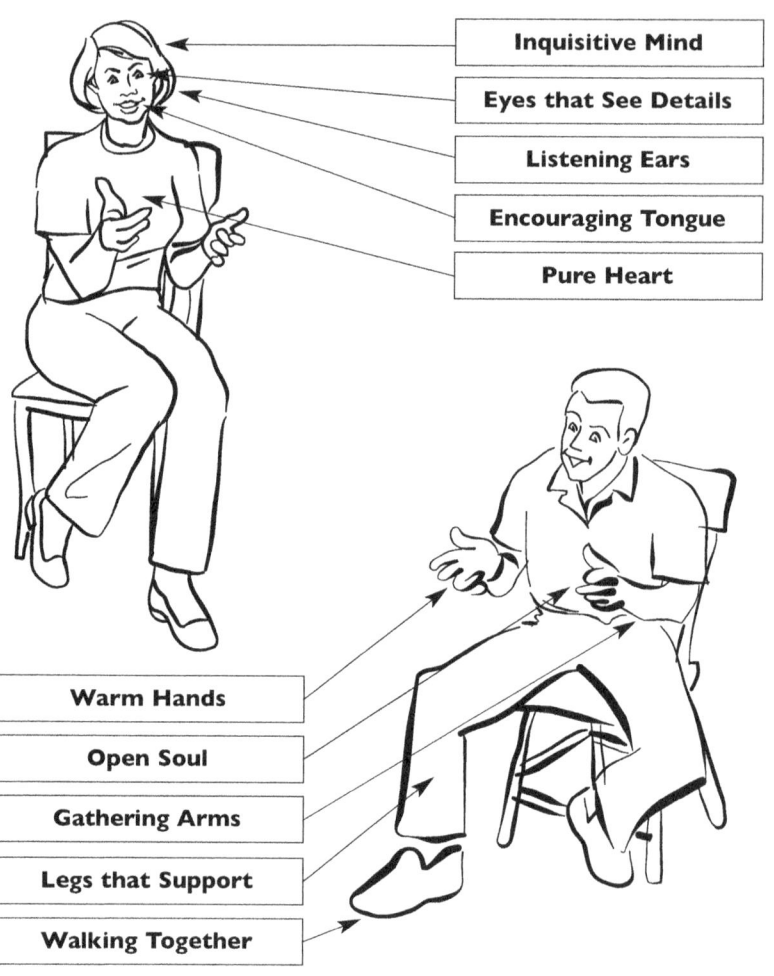

There are several different ways that this book can be used:

1. Start at the beginning and read the entire book to get a complete picture of leading a great small group meeting. This is an excellent way to overview the basic skills or to sharpen the skills that you already have.

2. Skip to the chapter that addresses the areas where you need specific development. If you need help asking good questions, then feel free to turn to chapter five. If you are not sure how to include non-Christians in your group, then chapter eight will prove helpful.

3. Skim the book for helpful ideas and tips that you can use in your meeting. You will see many of these in the lists and in the sidebars.
4. Read through the book with other small group leaders and discuss what you are learning. You might even do this as a part of your small group leader training with your pastor.

Try This!

Find these for simple ideas and tidbits that you can implement this week. Some of them are so obvious that you will wonder why you didn't think of them yourself.

Insight

These explanations will show you the inside track of being a great small group leader with testimonies, stories, and quotes from the lives of experienced leaders.

Strategy

Sometimes you need a new way of doing things to get out of a rut. These proven strategies provide practical ways to break out and do something new in your group.

Dictionary

Small group leadership is not difficult, but sometimes we misunderstand what it really involves. Look for these sidebars to make sure that you are on the same page with what really makes a small group great.

Unique Features of This Book

Throughout the book you will find tips and practical advice that will help you understand the principles of a great meeting and show you how to implement them in your group. You will find four special tips in the sidebars (pictured on the facing page).

A Companion Tool

How to Lead a Great Small Group Meeting will help you effectively guide your weekly meeting. But what do effective leaders do between the meetings? I have written a companion resource called *Home Cell Group Explosion: How Your Small Group Can Grow and Multiply* which explains what effective small group leaders do during the other six days and 22 hours. These two volumes work hand-in-hand to help you fully enter the ministry God has set before you.

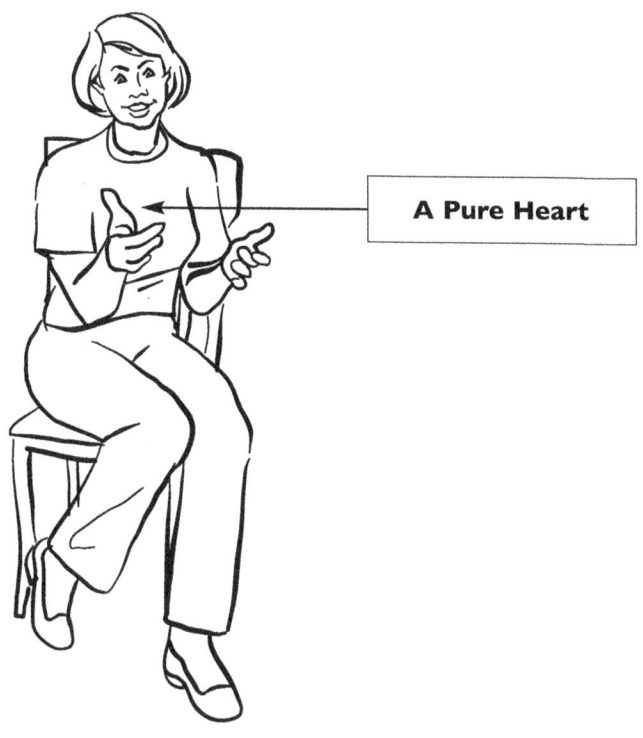

A Pure Heart

A Pure Heart

Small group leadership begins with heart preparation. A heart that is pure before God is the only foundation for leading a small group meeting. Without a heart for God, the meeting consists of only dry routines and rituals.

Chapter One

A Pure Heart:
Prepare Yourself

A certain winsomeness characterizes dynamic small group leaders. They demonstrate loving concern, but they firmly lead. They allow discus-sion to flow naturally, but refuse to stray from the theme. They listen intently, but won't allow one person to dominate the meeting. They build community, but not at the expense of reaching out to the unsaved. They take responsibility for the group, but refuse to do everything. They pro-mote group identity but never at the expense of the multiplication of new small groups.

Does this balance sound difficult? Let's just say it's *impossible* apart from the work of the Holy Spirit. Logic and technique, while necessary, can't teach the when and how of small group dynamics. Effective small group leadership begins with a transformed heart. The Holy Spirit works inside of the small group leader so he or she can minister from the overflow of the heart.

To successfully navigate the uncharted waters that lie ahead, you'll need a guide who knows the way. Jesus said, "But when he, the Spirit of truth, comes, *he will guide you* into all truth. He will not speak on his own; he will speak only what he hears, and he will tell you what is yet to come" (John 16:13).

You don't fully understand the tears and fears of Joan or the ambitions and dreams of John. When Joan, John, and the rest of the group arrive in your living room, the chemistry is unpredictable. You can know all the practices and techniques of small group dynamics and fail to meet the deep needs of the group. You need a guide . . . the Holy Spirit.

When to Stop Preparing for Your Meeting

Do yourself and your group a favor. Cease all *small group meeting preparation* at least one-half hour before it begins (e.g., lesson plans, refreshment preparation, etc.). Take that time to prepare your heart before God, asking Him to fill you with the Spirit. So many unexpected things happen in the course of a normal small group: the ringing phone, the unexpected non-Christian visitor, the forgetfulness of Susan to prepare the icebreaker, the broken guitar string, and John's job loss. When John shares about getting fired during the icebreaker, should you pray for him immediately, give him more opportunity to share, or wait until after the lesson (perhaps you know John has the tendency to talk a lot)? You'll need the Spirit's wisdom.

If you're a veteran small group leader, you know plans and preparation can help, but they're insufficient. You'll agree that Spirit-anointed common sense will hit the home runs. Following rigid, preconceived plans when someone is hurting results in a strikeout. To win the game, you need a good coach. The great news is that the Holy

Steps to the Spirit's Filling

➤ Ask for a fresh filling of the Holy Spirit. "If you then, though you are evil, know how to give good gifts to your children, how much more will your Father in heaven give the Holy Spirit to those who ask him!" (Luke 11:13). Jesus says, "Ask and it will be given to you; seek and you will find; knock and the door will be opened to you. For everyone who asks receives; he who seeks finds; and to him who knocks, the door will be opened" (Luke 11:9-10).

➤ Confess all known sin. David says, "If I had cherished sin in my heart, the Lord would not have listened" (Psalm 66:18).

➤ Be filled with the Spirit on a daily basis. In Ephesians 5:18, Paul says, ". . . be filled with the Spirit." The phrase "be filled" in the Greek points to a continual, *constant* filling. It's a daily thing.

Spirit is willing to give to you the inside, play-by-play counsel on a moment-by-moment basis. To hear His voice loud and clear when you need it, you'll need His filling before the meeting begins.

Some of the most powerful ministry occurs while chomping on chips or eating cookies after the meeting. Heart talk often transpires when our guard is down, and we're not worried about every detail of the small group meeting. The Spirit might stir you to minister to the newcomer or talk with the wayward. You might feel impressed to speak to Johnny, who rarely speaks during the meeting. Or maybe you just need to listen, while others lead the conversation.

Stay in tune with Him, and He'll make your way prosperous. He'll guide your steps.

God's Anointing

The best advice is from John the apostle: "As for you, the anointing you received from him remains in you, and you do not need anyone to teach you. But as his anointing teaches you about all things and as that anointing is real, not counterfeit — just as it has taught you, remain in him" (1 John 2:27).

Follow Christ's Example

Charles Hummel, a godly Christian leader, once wrote a classic article called, "The Tyranny of the Urgent." His basic thesis was that we live in constant tension between the urgent and the important. The important is our relationship with Jesus while the urgent is that which steals our time from God. Stephen Covey highlights this same tension in *The 7 Habits of Highly Effective People*:

> Urgent matters . . . press on us; they insist on action. They're often popular with others. They're usually right in front of us. And often they are pleasant, easy, fun to do. But so often they are unimportant! Important matters [that] are not urgent require more initiative, more proactivity . . . If we don't have a clear idea of what is important, of the results we desire in our lives, we are easily diverted into responding to the urgent.[1]

Be assured that urgent needs will crowd your schedule and spoil your initiative to spend time with God, unless you plan for and make your meeting with Him a priority. My counsel is to plan at least one day in advance when you will meet with Him. You might say, "I will meet God at 5:30 P.M. tomorrow or during my lunch break."

All of us have the same 24 hour day, including the President of the United States. If spending time with God is important, you'll make time for it. If it's not, you'll constantly offer excuses for not doing it.

Christ made decisions after communing with the Father. As we read in Luke 5:16, He made it a priority to spend time alone with His Father: ". . . Jesus often withdrew to lonely places and prayed." Luke 5:15 explains that when Christ's fame was spreading, the success of his ministry compelled Him to spend more time with God. In the midst of an increasingly busy ministry, He separated from the multitude for quiet time. If Jesus Christ, our model, prioritized His time with the Father, shouldn't we?

Rut Repair

David Yonggi Cho, pastor of Yoido Full Gospel Fellowship, sends his small group leaders to Prayer Mountain to fast and pray for a few days when the leader's small group is not growing. Have you ever made a trip to your own "prayer mountain?"

As a small group leader, spending time with God must be your chief priority. When your group senses you're hearing from God, they'll be more apt to follow you. When you can point to times in which you sensed His urging, and He spoke to your heart, you'll gain the respect of those in your group.

The Key to Success

My survey of 700 small group leaders revealed that the leader's success depended upon how much time he or she spent in daily devotions.

The Father's Reward

Jesus asks us to spend time in the Father's presence, but He also promises the Father's reward. Jesus says, "But when you pray, go into your room, close the door and pray to your Father, who is unseen. Then your Father, who sees what is done in secret, will reward you" (Matthew 6:6). The beauty of this reward is that you don't have to publicize it. You don't have to tell others how much time you spend in personal devotions. The Heavenly Father, who takes note of the time spent, will graciously reward you openly. In Genesis 15, Abraham refused the outward reward and adulation from the king of Sodom. God responded, "Do not be afraid, Abram. I am your shield, your very great reward."

Our heavenly Father is prepared to abundantly bless those who seek Him. Remember what the Scripture says: "Now to him who is able to do immeasurably more than all we ask or imagine, according to his power that is at work within us" (Ephesians 3:20). He'll do exceedingly and abundantly above all you can ask or think, if you make Him first in your life.

More than Techniques

This book emphasizes the importance of small group techniques. Yet, in this chapter, I've warned you not to follow techniques too closely. I've written, "Let the Spirit guide you." "Be open to analyze each situation with Spirit-anointed common sense." Sound like a contradiction? Not really. Plans, techniques and diligent preparation for the small group meeting are exceedingly important. Just don't allow them to control you. That's the Spirit's job. As you spend time in His presence, you'll make better plans, know how to handle each situation, and meet the needs of those present.

Sensitivity to the Spirit

What's the best way to minister to the hurting in times of grief? There's no right way. You just do your best to empathize with the hurts and weakness of others. You must trust the Holy Spirit.

The 7-Day, 7-Minute Prayer Experiment

If you're struggling with your feelings toward another person, begin with a seven-day prayer experiment. Pray seven minutes each day for your heart to change toward that person and let God resolve the conflict!

Points to Remember

Great small group leadership begins with a heart immersed in Christ and filled with the Holy Spirit. If your heart isn't right, then no list of techniques can lead your group into the things God has ahead. Remember:

➤ Stop preparing small group meeting details at least one-half hour before the meeting starts in order to spend time with God.
➤ Prioritize your daily devotional life in order to hear from God.
➤ Depend on God more than techniques.

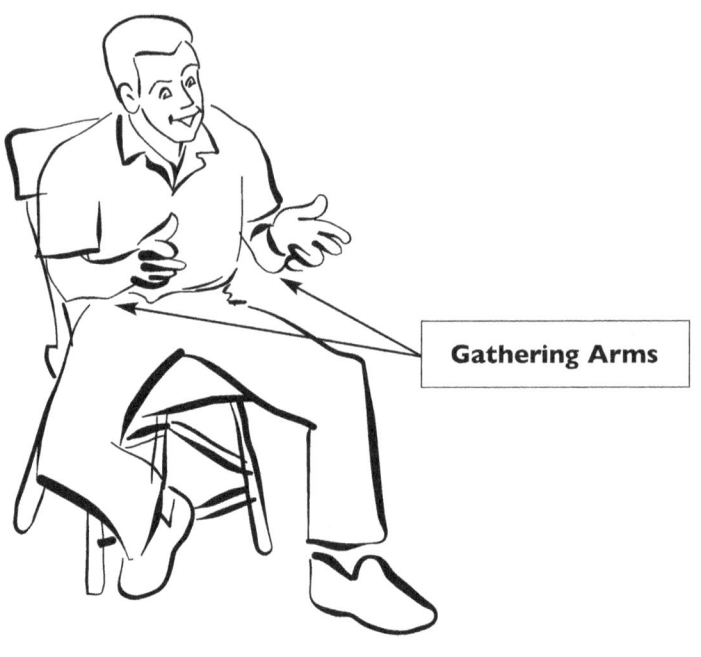

Gathering Arms

Gathering Arms

Just like the arms gather and hold things together, a proven small group strategy will help the small group leader gather people from the initial welcome time to the closing prayer. While the Holy Spirit might guide the small group meeting in unexpected ways, He expects the small group leader to have a plan.

Chapter Two

Gathering Arms:
How to Structure a Meeting

Monica arrived early for our small group and said, "I'm so thankful I'm no longer living with Andy. I feel clean inside, but it's still so hard; at times, I feel like I need him." Frank and Kathy arrived in the middle of our conversation and added their own thoughts.

The Holy Spirit showed me that we needed to go deeper, rather than abruptly restarting the small group meeting with an icebreaker. Tuning in to Monica's struggles and desiring to help her, each of us shared how God had delivered us from similar bondages. My intended lesson topic covered anger, but I decided to talk about freedom from bondage through the power of the Holy Spirit. God moved in a mighty way that night.

On this particular occasion, I felt moved by the Holy Spirit to scrap my plans because of a unique situation. However, I did have a plan. Ninety percent of the time, I'll follow that plan. You might also feel impressed to change your plans and do something unique — just make sure you have a strategy for your small group. Great small group meetings begin well and end well. They function like our arms, connecting everything together in an appealing way.

Some small group agendas are better than others. The best agenda I've discovered is called the 4Ws: *Welcome, Worship, Word, and Works* (or *Witness*). I like this order so much because it allows the group:

➤ To experience the *one anothers* of Scripture. The *Welcome* time enhances the open sharing of our personal lives.

➤ To enter the presence of God. We approach God through the *Worship* time and receive His fullness.
➤ To interact with God's Word; God speaks to us through the *Word*.
➤ To reach non-Christians; The *Works* time helps the group focus on outsiders.

The four Ws will not automatically produce life in your small group. They will, however, enhance God's work among the members of your group.

Introducing the 4Ws

Welcome — 15 minutes
Most small group members are tired when they arrive at the group. They've worked hard all day and probably don't feel like *being spiritual.* Some will attend because they know they *should* be there, not because they *feel like attending.* Begin on a joyful note. Let them ease into group life.

The *Welcome* time normally begins with a dynamic question that breaks the ice. The best icebreakers guarantee a response. You can buy entire books on lively icebreakers, so you shouldn't experience a shortage in this area.

Most people know us by our profession. We're known as a teacher, construction worker, doctor, housewife, etc. A great icebreaker stirs us to talk about our hobbies, family backgrounds, or personal experiences. The icebreaker draws the group together in a family atmosphere.

Confessions of a Tired Small Group Member

One man who has attended my small group for over one year confessed to the group, "Every Thursday night I wrestle with my feelings about coming to the group. After an intense day of working ten hours, I'd rather space out in front of the TV or play on my computer. I come because God always ministers to me here, and I'm growing in my Christian faith."

Cool Icebreakers

➤ Who was your favorite grade school teacher and why?
➤ When you are stressed or frustrated about something what do you do?
➤ What's the best thing that happened in your life last year?
➤ What is your hobby and why do you like it?
➤ Who was most influential in your own decision to follow Christ? What was that person's relationship to you (friend, parent, teacher, etc.)?
➤ Ask each person to complete the sentence: "One word to describe me is . . ."
➤ What is one of the most important pieces of advice someone has given you?
➤ Describe your week in colors.
➤ What animal best describes your mood right now?
➤ How forgiving are you when a friend lets you down?

Some small groups even provide a light snack during the *Welcome* time (people feel more socially inclined with a chip in one hand and a soft drink in the other). This is a great idea, if you're not on a tight budget. However, don't neglect the closing refreshment time.

➤ *Evaluation Question:* When you've finished the *Welcome Time*, are group members more comfortable with each other and ready to enjoy being together?

How to start the Icebreaker

Pointer: Don't start the meeting by saying "The ice breaker for tonight is . . ." Rather, you could start by saying, "Think of a time . . ."

Worship — 20 minutes
The goal of the *Worship* time is to enter the presence of the living God and to give Him control of the meeting. The worship time helps the group go beyond socializing. Without Christ's presence, the small group is no different than a work party, a

27

family gathering, or a gathering of friends at a football game.

Entering God's presence through song is an important part of the worship time. Make sure everyone can read or see the words. Why?

➤ First-time visitors will feel uncomfortable without seeing the words.

➤ Some new Christians or church members don't know the worship choruses of your church.

➤ You'll have more liberty to sing new songs.

You don't have to play guitar or sing like a recording artist to lead God-honoring worship. I've experienced worship times in which the members choked out a joyful *noise* (emphasis on the word *noise*). God doesn't require a tabernacle choir. He looks at the motivation for singing. Some small groups prefer to watch or listen to a YouTube worship video.[2]

The worship leader should choose three to four songs *before* the worship starts. Or, the worship leader might invite small group members to select the songs *before* the worship time and then sing them in sequence. I think it's best to concentrate on God during the entire worship time, rather than stopping and starting to pick the next song. I like to intermingle praise and prayer between songs.

Let everyone see the words

It's more relaxing if each person has his or her own song sheet or can see the words on a screen. Trying to hold a song sheet steady for someone else to see (when your hands are shaking) might be an unforgettable experience-- but not necessarily a positive one.

Don't limit the *Worship Time* to singing songs. One small group leader told me, "It's important to go beyond singing songs. Our group has experienced God's presence through reading Psalms together, praying sentence prayers, or even waiting in silence."

➤ *Evaluation Question:* When your group finishes the worship time, is the group focused on Christ and ready for Him to minister to the group?

Worship Ideas[3]

Spend a few minutes glorifying God by using the alphabet to describe His attributes. Examples:

A - awesome, all mighty, authority
B - bright morning star, beautiful, boundless
C - compassionate, caring
D - devoted, deep, desirous
E - everlasting, exalted
F - forever, friend, faithful
G - great, gracious
H - holy, high tower
I - infinite, indescribable, inclusive
J - just, jealous, joy
K - king, keystone, knowing
L - loving, loyal, long-suffering
M - mighty, manifest, magnificent
N - near, noble, noteworthy
O - omnipresent (all present), omnipotent (all powerful), only
P - priceless, partner, parent
Q - quantity, quality
R - righteous, redeemer
S - strong, shelter
T - true, tireless
U - understanding, unwavering
V - victorious, vanquisher, vast
W - willing, wise, warrior
X - x's out my sin, examiner, x-ray (have fun with these!)
Y - yardstick, yes
Z - zealous, zenith

After you have worked your way through the alphabet ask the group to now praise God for being king, or victorious, or holy in their lives. Encourage every person to pray a short sentence prayer of praise. For example, "I praise you God for being my high tower, the shelter in a storm."

Checklist for Worship Preparation

➤ **Be Prepared.** If possible, play or sing through the songs before the meeting begins.

➤ **Be Confident.** Never apologize for leading. If you make a mistake, keep on moving. Expertise is not a requirement in leading worship. People don't expect perfection.

➤ **Be Sensitive.** Leading worship requires three sets of ears: physical ears to hear how the music is progressing, mental ears to gauge the atmosphere of the group, and spiritual ears to hear what the Holy Spirit is saying.

➤ **Be Authentic.** Fix your eyes on Jesus, the author and perfecter of our faith (Hebrews 12:2). Don't let the action of leading worship become a distraction from your own worship. This works best when you're prepared.

➤ **Be Passionate.** Worship demands wholehearted participation. Become wholly engaged in the worship process as you lead.

➤ **Use Scripture.** The book of Psalms is an excellent resource for worship. Start by having somebody read a Psalm while the musician plays the first song in the background. Or, at a predetermined time, have somebody read a Scripture between songs.

➤ **Be Positive.** Focus on the character of God (holiness, love, power, etc.). This is not the time to browbeat people into a more authentic faith. Let the Holy Spirit do His own convicting. Choose songs that bring people into close relationship with God. Avoid songs with distracting tunes or confusing lyrics.

➤ *Practice Continuity.* Worship should flow as seamlessly as possible with everything else that is happening. Try to not pause in between songs, but move right into the next one if possible.

➤ *Finish Well.* It's best to ease out of worship rather than just abruptly ending it (e.g. Have people pray words of exaltation and worship).

Small Group Resource Material

➤ Joel Comiskey Group features a daily blog, videos, and hundreds of articles: www.joelcomiskeygroup.com
➤ Small Group Network, an online website dedicated to small groups, provides bountiful resources: www.smallgroups.com
➤ TOUCH Outreach Ministries publishes articles and curriculum about small group ministry: www.touchusa.org
➤ The Navigators are famous for their excellent small group material: www.navpress.com

Word— *40 minutes*

The *Word* time is when God speaks to our hearts through the Bible. Resources abound to help you prepare a top-notch lesson. One of the best resources is the *Serendipity Bible for Groups*.

Many small groups follow the same theme and Scripture as the Sunday message. Even if this is the case, it's best NOT to discuss the sermon. The people should interact with God's Word, not with the sermon. If the sermon itself is the reference point, visitors and those who missed the sermon will feel isolated.

Even though the church provides the lesson, it's essential that each small group leader examine the lesson and apply it according to the needs of the group.

Without fail, God speaks to the group through His Word and people recognize their needs. I find it very effective to ask for specific prayer requests after the lesson time. Often we'll lay hands on those with special needs. I like to take the last ten minutes of the *Word* time to pray for the specific needs of the group.

➤ *Evaluation Questions:* Did the group share honestly and manifest vulnerability before one another? Did the group learn how to walk more obediently with Christ during the week?

Prayer Time Suggestions

➤ Never force someone to pray. The fear of praying out loud could keep someone from returning to your group. Don't needlessly offend someone in this area.

➤ Teach about prayer. For many people, prayer is a new experience. Explain why we pray and to whom we direct our prayers. It's best that you exemplify prayer before asking the group to pray.

➤ Focus on prayer requests.

➤ After the lesson, it's good to close in a time of silent prayer, as each person examines his or her heart. Then ask the group for petitions. Ask certain members in the group to pray for those petitions, making sure you don't ask newcomers to pray out loud.

Six Kinds of Small Group Prayers

➤ **Subject Prayers:** One person prays out loud, everyone else agrees with what is prayed. Others are free to add prayer about the current subject when no one is praying. This is a great opportunity for the group to discipline themselves to really agree with one another in prayer, not just listen.

➤ **Short Prayers:** Pray only prayers one to three sentences long.

➤ **Simple Prayers:** Prayers don't need to be long to be powerful. The leader must emphasize that prayer doesn't need to be complicated.

➤ **Specific Prayers:** We should ask for specific things since God answers in specific ways.

➤ **Silent Prayers:** Prayer can mean sitting in silence before God, relaxing, enjoying Him.

➤ **Spirit Prayers:** This type of prayer is birthed in the heart of God and then revealed to us.

Works — 15 minutes

The last part of the small group, the *Works* time (or *Witness* time), helps us focus on others. There is no "one way" to do this. The main thought that should guide this time is OUTREACH. The type of outreach might vary on a weekly basis:

➤ Praying for non-Christians to invite
➤ Preparing a social project
➤ Planning for multiplication
➤ Deciding on the next outreach event for the small group (e.g., dinner, video, picnic, etc.)
➤ Praying for non-Christian families

A possible dialogue about evangelism might look like this:

Leader: "George, who will you invite next week?"

George: "I'll invite my neighbor."

Leader: "Great, let's pray in a moment that George's neighbor responds to the invitation."

Ideas for Reaching Out

➤ Post an ad in a local hardware store advertising free services from group members.
➤ Offer free services to targeted people (like changing oil in single moms' cars).
➤ Set up a table at the local store that offers information on how to drug-proof teenagers.
➤ Offer to mow the lawn for someone new in the neighborhood where the small group is located.

Leader: "Julie, who are you going to invite next week?"

The leader might ask the group, "Remember to pray for our new multiplication in two months. Pray for Frank, who needs to complete the last training course. Pray that he'll be ready to start a new small group."

During this time, you might promote and plan a social outreach project. I'm convinced that small groups are perfectly positioned to meet the physical needs of those both inside and outside the group. A small group offers a unique, effective way to reach deeply into the heart of a non-Christian person. The New Testament church grew and prospered through need-oriented group evangelism. God is calling His Church back to this exciting method of outreach.

➤ *Other ideas:* Reach out to the community by visiting a retirement home, ministering to street kids, or helping out in an orphanage.

➤ *Evaluation Question:* Is Jesus working through us to reach others?

Were the People Edified?

During the ministry to Monica that I shared at the beginning of this chapter, I sensed the need to talk about the Holy Spirit's filling and His power to deliver us from sin. We examined several passages that

Inviting Non-Christians

Question: I have eight people in my small group who have been members of the church for years, but they don't want to reach out to unbelievers. What do I do?

Answer: These people likely have discovered community, which is a good thing. But they fear that if they include others, they will lose that sense of community. The irony of their reaction is that the only way to retain community is to give it away. Small groups that do not regularly add new life eventually dry up and die. When a small group tries to maintain what it has, the life-giving power of the Spirit leaves. The small group sooner or later withers.[4]

How to Reach Out as a Group

Each small group could care for one shut-in from the church. You can send cards on birthdays and special occasions, provide a visit at least monthly, bring a meal and eat with them, and bring families (children included) when appropriate. If there are many shut-ins in your church, each family unit could take one as their care-burden.[5]

Example of an Outreach Project

Steve Sjogren's book *Conspiracy of Kindness* provides excellent examples of group outreach. Here are some examples:

➤ Hold a free car wash.
➤ In teams of two, canvass a neighborhood and offer free batteries for smoke detectors.
➤ On a bike path, check bike tires for air and adjust pressure if necessary.
➤ Take free Polaroid pictures at a park.

When people ask why, just say "It's just our way of showing God's love in a practical way — no strings attached."

referred to the Spirit's willingness to fill us. We concluded the lesson on our knees, seeking the Prince of Peace to fill us. My wife and I then went around and laid hands on Monica, Frank, and Kathy praying for them to be filled with the Spirit of God. Afterwards, Frank blurted out, "How did you know I needed that lesson? It was just for me!"

Edification literally means "to build up or construct." Paul says to the Corinthian church, "What then shall we say, brothers? When you come together, everyone has a hymn, or a word of instruction, a revelation, a tongue or an interpretation. All of these must be done for the strengthening [edifying] of the church" (1 Corinthians 14:26).

The issue of building-up should be the guiding principle of the small group. A successful small group meeting is one in which everyone is built up and encouraged in the faith.

Practical Steps for Edification in the Small Group

➤ The small group leader must be transparent and model what he expects others to follow.
➤ Cultivate a safe environment for those needing edification.
➤ Ask the members to become a vessel used by God to edify others.
➤ Point the one being edified back to God.

The standard for success is whether or not Christ's body went away edified — not whether or not you fulfilled the 4Ws.

Focus on Christ

The focus of your small group must be Jesus Christ. Some want to convert the group into a Bible study, others an evangelistic crusade, and still others a worship concert. Some don't think it's a *real* small group unless someone delivers a red-hot prophesy.

Lift Christ high in your group, and He'll give you a gentle balance of study, worship, evangelism, and fellowship. Perhaps one week you'll spend more time in the Word, while another week you'll dive into worship.

Remember the 4Ws are not four laws. They're guidelines to help you focus on Jesus and maximize participation. Focusing on the presence, power, and purposes of Christ in your midst helps provide the proper balance.

Points to Remember

Having an orderly small group agenda won't guarantee success in your small group. It will, however, link together essential small group values such as sharing, the Word, evangelism, and worship. Like gathering arms, a proven structure will provide continuity and purpose. Remember these points for success:

➤ Great small group meetings follow a predictable — but not legalistic —pattern:
  • *Welcome* (relationship building)
  • *Worship* (entering the presence of God)
  • *Word* (applying God's Word to your lives)
  • *Works* (reaching out to others)
➤ Measure the meeting by:
  • Were the people edified?
  • Was Christ glorified?

No Two Meetings Alike

The Love Alive Church in Tegucigalpa, Honduras asks its leaders to creatively vary the order of the meeting each week. The reason? To avoid monotony and maximize creativity.

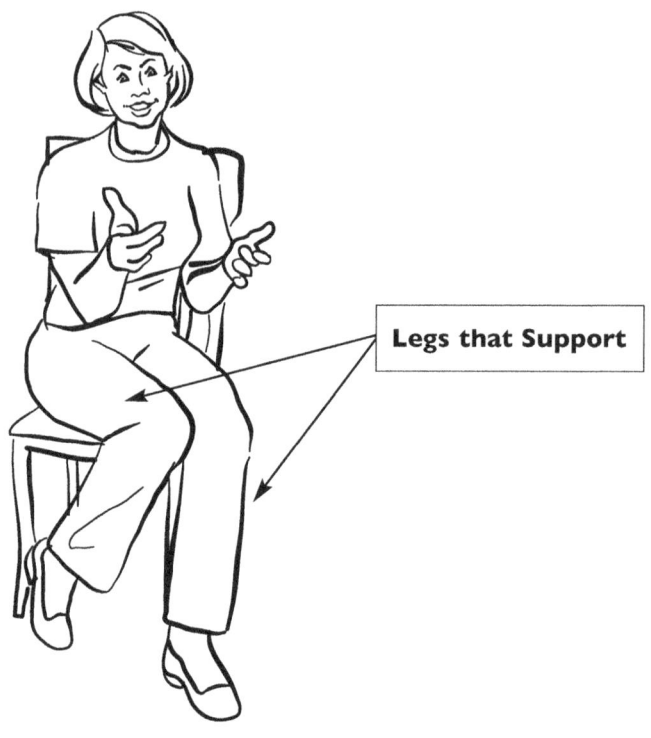

Legs that Support

Legs that Support

Our legs support our entire body and allow us to walk, run, and jump. Small group facilitation supports group members by empowering them to exercise their spiritual muscles, apply the Word of God to their lives, and minister to one another.

Chapter Three

Legs that Support: Facilitating Others

Fred diligently prepared all week for his Thursday night group.[1] At that time, I knew little about small group ministry, and I fully expected a Bible study, complete with exegesis, opinions from commentators, and illustrations. To my astonishment, Fred spoke very little that night. He skillfully drew the information from us. Although he had scrutinized the Bible passage, he led us to dig up the treasures for ourselves. He peppered us with questions that forced us to delve deeper and deeper into the text.

I left that meeting with a new appreciation for the power of participation in Bible study. I discovered that diligent lesson preparation and open sharing are not mutually exclusive.

Group Participation

Robert Wuthnow, who along with George Gallup conducted a national research project on small groups in the United States, concluded, "Leaders . . . function best when they are sensitive to the dynamics of the group, steer the discussion, encourage members to participate, and help to keep things running smoothly rather than dominating the discussion themselves."[2]

Fred empowered us to discover God's Word for ourselves. Like strong legs propelling the body onwards, Fred exemplified how facilitators can encourage others to participate.

Years later I made an unexpected visit to another small group. During the lesson, the leader rattled off numerous Greek words. "Is she trying to impress me with her knowledge?" I thought to myself. She liberally quoted Bible commentators and ended up teaching 90 percent of the lesson.

When others dared to comment, she hesitantly acknowledged them. Quickly, however, she cut them off, preferring her own authoritative voice. "These poor, bottled-up group members," I mused. "They want so badly to share their souls."

Facilitators Refuse to Preach and Teach

During the summer of 1981, I was working a few odd jobs, trying to pay for my last year of Bible school. I asked the pastor of my home church in Long Beach, California if I could lead a Bible study (I yearned to show off my newly acquired Bible school knowledge!). Every Tuesday night, I gathered a group of people in the small church bookstore and taught them the Word of God. I didn't prepare questions, nor did I expect those attending to participate. During those same summer months, I preached numerous times on Sunday morning. God provided opportunities for me to use my budding gifts.

Perhaps you are called to teach or preach. Look for opportunities to use your gifts. Just remember that the small group meeting is not one of those occasions. Your job is to kindle participation among the group members. The small group focus is the personal application of Bible knowledge to daily life. This emphasis digs deeper than hearing information. It's a time when confession, inner healing, transparent sharing, and renewal happen.

I visited two different young professional small groups within the same month. In one, I soared away from the meeting edified both socially and spiritually. The icebreaker fulfilled its purpose — it broke down walls of indifference and helped us get to know each other better. The worship carried us into God's presence and filled our deep longing for God Himself. The leader guided each member to participate in the small group lesson. All of us explored God's Word together. Afterwards, each member expressed personal needs in the prayer time. Finally, the small group members gathered around the refreshment table to interact socially — laughing and sharing.

In the other group, the leader clung to the mini-service mentality. He cut the icebreaker short and left everyone hanging. After worship, we opened our Bibles. With a Bible in one hand and a document that looked like a manuscript in the other, the leader proceeded to dominate the meeting for the next 40 minutes.

I felt for the young people who were forced to sit through another service. He answered his own questions and even controlled the concluding prayer time.

This leader, like many, was so comfortable hearing his own voice that he kept on talking and talking. Several times, I felt compelled to break into the meeting and open it up for discussion, but I controlled myself, not wanting to embarrass the leader. I left that night feeling "bottled up."

Facilitators Empower Others

The root definition of facilitate is "to make easy." The facilitator is the group's servant, empowering the members to enjoy God and each other. Rather than lording over the group, the facilitator washes their feet, ministering to them at every opportunity.[3]

The 70-30 Principle

The small group leader talks only 30 percent, while the small group members share 70 percent of the time. This should be the goal of every small group leader!

Small group facilitators encourage group members to speak what's on their minds. They gently remind the group to empower each other through active listening. The goal of the small group is to strengthen others through mutual edification.

The facilitator might ask, "What do the rest of you think?" All members are asked to fill in the blanks and add new dimensions. After everyone has taken a turn, the facilitator summarizes the comments of the group.

Synonyms for Facilitate

Help, Aid, Assist, Ease, Make Easy, Empower, Lubricate, Smooth, Make Possible.

Communication in a classroom takes place between student and teacher (question-answer). The teacher imparts information while the students take notes. Communication in a small group flows among all

Celyce Comiskey's Small Group

"I couldn't get them to stop talking," my wife told me as she reflected on her small group for young mothers. "Everyone wanted to share personal struggles, and it was so hard to bring it back to the Bible. There's such a great hunger to share."

members. Elizabeth, a member of the small group, feels just as free to direct her comments to John, a group member, as she does to Jane, the group facilitator. Often the facilitator simply observes the communication that's taking place.

The facilitator is not stiff and passive — only listening and not sharing. A facilitator interacts just like other group members, sharing personal reflections, experiences, and modeling transparency.

Like Fred in the opening illustration, facilitators diligently mine the riches of God's Word for the purpose of empowering the members to discover God's treasure for themselves. They know the basics of inductive Bible study, but the fruit of their study results in increased participation.

Facilitators Need Support

When I first started leading a small group, I attended a very large church. The small group pastor met with all potential Bible study leaders. I was already leading a small group (which he didn't know about), so I met with him. He blessed my activity, and that was the last time I heard from him. I didn't receive pastoral care, training, or help in preparing the lessons. In reality, I was leading an independent small group which acted like a house church (at times, forty people attended).

Inductive Bible Study

Inductive Bible study takes place when a person draws conclusions from a Bible verse or verses based on its plain meaning, rather than simply accepting an explanation from a commentary or an outside Bible authority.

In those days, I felt it was unspiritual to prepare my "Bible study" beforehand because I didn't want to "quench the Spirit." Before the meeting began, I simply received the "Word from God" for the group. Then during the lesson time I opened my mouth, hoping God would fill it. Well, He did fill it, but often with the same things I had shared the previous week. I'll never forget the night my good friend and co-leader, Bob Burtch, took me aside and said, "Joel, you have a lot of talents and abilities, but Bible teaching is not one of them."

Small group leaders need support to be successful. If you're currently leading a small group, I hope you have someone watching over you. If not, ask your senior pastor to periodically meet with you. Small group leaders need to interact with more experienced leaders. Learn from the growing small group-driven churches around the world. They don't allow small group leaders to work alone; they provide close support and contact.

Facilitators Learn while Leading

Don't wait too long to use your gifts and talents. You can't grow unless you exercise your muscles along the way.

A farmer wanted to enter the world of horse racing, so he bought a beautiful race horse. Everyday he cleaned the horse and groomed it. He didn't want to exercise the horse for fear of wearing it out, so he used his faithful mule to perform the farm chores. On the day of the big race, his prize horse could hardly move. Its muscles were flabby and atrophied. The farmer had no other choice except to enter his mule for the big race.

House Church versus Small Group-based Church

➤ **House Church:** A community of 8-40 people who meet together on a weekly basis. Each House Church is independent. While some House Churches belong to networks, many do not recognize any further structure beyond themselves.

➤ **Small Group-driven Church:** Small groups are intimately linked to the life of the local church. Those who attend the small groups are expected to attend the congregational gatherings (normally on Sunday). Those who attend congregational gatherings are expected to attend a small group.

Don't sit on the sidelines, waiting for the big race. People learn best while practicing what they're learning. Some think it's best to wait until they *really* know the Bible. "You'll never have enough Bible knowledge," I tell them. "Even recognized, highly skilled Bible teachers are learning continually."

Others think they must wait until they're ready to answer all questions. "You don't need to answer every question," I tell them. In fact, I encourage this response to difficult questions: "I'm not sure how to answer that question, but I'm going to look into it this week, and I'll get back to you." This humble stance will generate confidence between you and your small group members. During the week, you can study the Bible, read Bible commentaries, and go to your coach or pastor to ask for help.

Two Essential Qualities of Facilitators

What skills are necessary to lead a group? At least two: They're summed up in the great commandments — love God and love your neighbor. All small group leaders must abundantly possess these two attributes.

Variety of Gifts Among Small Group Leaders

When I polled 700 small group leaders in eight countries, I discovered that no particular gift distinguished those who could multiply their group from those who could not. Here's how the small group leaders viewed their own giftedness:

- Teaching — 25.1%
- Leadership — 20.3%
- Evangelism — 19.0%
- Pastoral care — 10.6%
- Mercy — 10.6%
- Other — 14.4%

No one particular gift stood out as more important. There was no one particular gift of the Spirit (such as evangelism) that distinguished those who could multiply their groups from those who could not. Additionally, small group leaders with the gift of teaching were no more prone to multiply their group than those with the gift of mercy.

Sincere Love for God

Jesus, God's Son, said, "Love the Lord your God with all your heart and with all your soul and with all your mind and with all your strength" (Mark 12:30). No one has arrived at the stage of loving God completely. The key questions are: Are you growing in your love relationship with Jesus Christ? Are you enjoying His love letter to you on a daily basis? God uses people who are growing in love with Him.

Sincere Love for Others

Jesus followed the first command with a second: "Love your neighbor as yourself. There is no commandment greater than these" (Mark 12:31). The time-tested, oft-quoted phrase still rings true, *People don't care how much you know until they know how much you care.* Your success as a small group leader depends on your love for your small group members. More than any other attribute, God uses leaders who care. Anyone can successfully lead a small group — if he or she is willing to love people.

Remember to Facilitate!

Remember Fred? He fervently studied the Scripture in order to facilitate participation. He empowered others by giving them a chance to apply the Scriptures to their lives. Facilitators like Fred refuse to convert the small group into another church service. The wares of the facilitator's craft are application-oriented, Bible-related questions, a listening ear, and loving concern.

Common Excuses for not Leading a Small Group

➤ *Excuse #1:* "I have very little time."

All of us have the same amount of time to invest; the key question is how will you invest it.

➤ *Excuse #2:* "I haven't been trained."

The basic prerequisites for leading a small group include: Love for Jesus, Love for His Word, and a desire to minister to others. Small group leaders never feel they have enough knowledge. All small group leaders are growing and learning.

➤ *Excuse #3:* "I'm not mature enough in the Lord."

If you're a young Christian, hungry for Jesus, with a desire to serve Him, leading a small group will provide an important stepping stone in your spiritual growth.

Points to Remember

Our legs offer support and strength to the rest of the body. Likewise, the art of facilitation supports and encourages each member to participate. Effective small group leaders empower others to share and apply the lesson to their own lives. Remember:

➤ Facilitators refuse to preach and teach.
➤ Facilitators empower others.
➤ Facilitators need coaching.
➤ Facilitators learn while leading.
➤ Two essential qualities for facilitators are:
- Sincere love for God.
- Sincere love for others.

An Open Soul

An Open Soul

The soul is the gateway to the rest of the body. It's that immaterial part that reflects who we really are. Great small group leaders don't hide their souls behind superiority and superficiality. They share honestly and intimately, starting a chain reaction among the members.

Chapter Four

An Open Soul:
Practicing Transparency

"Joel, there are very few entryways into your life," my brother Andy said to me. "You have a tendency to make yourself look good — always putting your best foot forward. It's hard for people to relate to you," he said. The painful truth of my brother's words dug deep into my soul.

Andy knows the importance of an honest, transparent lifestyle. God delivered him from homosexuality 46 years ago. Now he and his wife Annette constantly magnify God's grace in their lives by helping others find healing from sexual brokenness. For Andy, this means sharing his testimony continually. Open and transparent communication helps him to minister God's grace to others. The words of my brother continue to speak to me. His counsel has stirred me to create entryways.

Synonyms for Entryway

Door, entrance, access, accessibility, means of approach.

Successful small group leaders open their heart and soul and allow others to see who they really are. They don't hide behind outward appearances and trumped-up images. They realize that by sharing weaknesses they actually gain strength. They create entryways that lead to more intimate group communion. My good friend, Bill Mangham, excels at transparency. Others feel relaxed in Bill's presence because they know he's real. Recently, Bill walked into my home and showed me two photos. One revealed his son successfully surfing a wave; the other showed Bill falling flat on his face, as he tried to do the same. "A typical example of Bill Mangham," I thought to myself. Bill creates friends by creating entryways. He doesn't try to impress others. In fact, I've never heard Bill boast about his accomplishments. He doesn't need to because they're so evident. Bill is respected by all and is constantly elevated to leadership positions.

Bare. Naked. This is the reality of our situation before God. The writer of Hebrews declares, "Nothing in all creation is hidden from God's sight. Everything is uncovered and laid bare before the eyes of him to whom we must give account" (4:13).

Actually, there's nothing in the Bible that talks about creating entryways. There are, however, many examples of transparent living before God.

Paul's Strength in Weakness

God's words to Paul, "My grace is sufficient for you, for my power is made perfect in weakness" (2 Cor. 12:9a).

Lead the Way

Group transparency will never happen unless the leader shares some of his or her deep struggles. David Hocking says, "Learn to admit your mistakes in the presence of the group and to apologize sincerely when things go wrong or do not turn out the way you expected . . . admitting failure in the midst of success is a key to good leadership. Learn to be open and honest before others. They'll love you for it (or at least fall over backwards out of shock!)."[1]

If the leader always wants to give the best impression, the other small group members will do likewise. Some leaders imagine they're promoting transparency, but their testimonies don't resonate with the members. "Pray for me, I'm really struggling. Normally, I spend two hours in daily prayer and Bible reading, but recently I've only spent one hour . . ." How will people react? "Yea, right, like she really needs our prayers . . ." Most likely the majority in the group struggle to spend 15 minutes in daily devotions!

Don't wait until you have a major problem to share. What about the small, daily difficulties we all face? The breakdown of your computer, the long wait in line, or the demanding schedule at work.

When my computer broke down, for example, I shared my

frustration with the group. "This has been a miserable week. I didn't reach a single objective. I was a slave to trying to get my computer running again." People could relate, and they saw me as a real person — as opposed to Pastor Comiskey! Ralph Neighbour says:

> We have found in small group life that group members will typically be as transparent and open as the leader is willing to be. In other words, group members will seldom "risk" transparency and openness until they have seen someone else take the same risk. . . . The question is whether God

would have all of us be open and vulnerable. Living in community means living in relationship, and living in relationship means vulnerability and transparency.[3]

Vulnerability

"Trust is built when we make ourselves vulnerable to others . . . Letting others know what we stand for, what we value, what we want, what we hope for, what we're willing (and not willing) to do means disclosing information about ourselves. That can be risky . . ." argue Kouzes and Posner.[2]

The First Step

Tell your story first. So often we make the mistake of asking the other person a question, and putting him on the spot. By disclosing something personal about yourself, you take the initial step toward creating trust.[4]

"I don't know how to model transparency," you say? "How do I begin?" Why don't you ask the members to pray for an area of weakness or struggle in your own life? When asking a question that requires vulnerability, share first, setting the model for others to follow.

You don't always need to share problems, fears, or weaknesses. What about your desires and plans? Transparency means talking about yourself in an honest way, allowing others to know your aspirations, dreams, and hopes.

Honest to Others

We've all experienced "fellowship" times when everybody tried to impress each other. You feel pressure to perform. True Christian fellowship, on the other hand, is transparent and honest. John says, ". . . if we walk in the light, as he is in the light, we have *fellowship* with one another, and the blood of Jesus, his Son, purifies us from all sin" (1 John 1:7).

John Wesley promoted open sharing as the cornerstone of his small group-based church in the eighteenth century. When Wesley died, he left behind a church of 100,000 members and 10,000 small groups. Wesley's small groups (called class meetings) normally lasted for one hour, and the main event was

Open Your Life to Others

Close relationships require intimacy. And intimacy demands vulnerability. Letting people know us at our point of need can be hard because we fear rejection if they find out about the "real" us.

Example of Frank & Kathy

Frank and Kathy were robbed at gunpoint while with their children. Four days later, Frank and Kathy attended our small group. We skipped the ice-breaker time, sang a few songs, and then dedicated the rest of the time to listening to them (as opposed to offering counsel). They spent 45 minutes unburdening their souls.

"reporting on your soul."[5] The class would open with a song. Then the leader would share a personal religious experience. Afterwards, he would inquire about the spiritual life of those in the group. The meeting was built upon the sharing of personal experience of the past week. Wesley's class meetings are best described by one word: "transparency."

Small groups shake with open, honest sharing. Walls of hurt crumble. Healing occurs. Churchgoers who get lost in the pews suddenly have a name and a face. Statistics on a church roll become a priest of the living God. Church comes to life as people open up in the small group and worship freely in the large group gathering.

Confess Your Faults to Each Other

James, writing to a group of believers, says, "Therefore confess your sins to each other and pray for each other so that you may be healed. The prayer of a righteous man is powerful and effective" (James 5:16). Healing takes place when we share our sins and weaknesses and then pray for one another. Mutual concern is the way to combat discouragement and downfall.

"I've stolen thousands of dollars from my company and they still don't know it," Nancy began. "My boss placed her confidence in me, and I deceived her." Nancy, a brand-new Christian, confessed this to the small group one night. "I know I must now go to them and confess what I did. I'm willing to go to jail, if necessary. Yet, I know that, even in jail, Jesus Christ will be with me." She asked us to pray for her, knowing that the next day she would confront her company's owners. We bore her burden, prayed for her that night, and dedicated ourselves to pray for her the next day.

She asked me to accompany her for moral support. As I sat and listened to Nancy's confession in front of the company's owners, my eyes filled with tears. "I stole money from you [$60,000]. Now that I'm a Christian I need to right this wrong. I'm willing to go to jail," she said.

It was an incredible testimony before these non-Christians. They were impressed. They asked her to pay back the money but were very gracious to her, even saying that they wanted to remain friends.

I admit discernment is needed. There's a time and a place for everything, and you don't need to share every detail of your life with everyone you meet. You also need to know that what you share will be kept confidential. What is shared in the group must not go beyond the group.

Although caution is in order, I've discovered that we as believers have the tendency to err on the conservative side. We expose too little of our lives, thus erecting barriers instead of creating entryways.

Tips for Small Group Disclosure

➤ Get to know one another.
➤ Maintain strict confidentiality among the group.
➤ Carry one another's burdens.
➤ Hold each other accountable.

Transformation

Transparency should lead to transformation. When a person or couple reveals a struggle, he or she is reaching out for help. "Pray for me." "Help me." The desired result is change. "We want to stop fighting and start understanding each other," the young couple shares. Such deep sharing springs from an earnest desire to change.

The small group should hold the couple accountable to improve their behavior — not in a legislative, legalistic way, but through constant encouragement. The writer of Hebrews had transformation in mind when saying, "Let us not give up meeting together, as some are in the habit of doing, but let us encourage one another — and all the more as you see the Day approaching" (10:25).

Transparency without transformation is superficial. I call it a *feelings time* or a *Love Boat* small group.

The person, having unburdened his soul, willfully goes right back into the mire. "I can't find time to have devotions," Jim shares. "I'm too busy." The leader might respond, "Let's pray for Jim." The group prays for transformation to take place and for Jim to see the need to place the living God before accomplishments. Yet, if Jim shares the same transparent confession week after week but doesn't take concrete steps to prioritize God in His schedule, it's right to assume he wants transparency without transformation.

Accountability in the Discipleship Groups of John Wesley

Questions asked at each Methodist band meeting:

➤ What known sins have you committed since the last meeting?
➤ What temptations have you met with?
➤ How were you delivered?
➤ What have you thought, said, or done which may or may not be sin?

Guide Your Group Into Deeper Levels of Communication

The members of your group will not open up all at once. There are steps to lead a group into deep levels of intimacy. During the initial stages, your group will share the latest weather, sports, events at

Small Group Transformation

"The priority of sanctification [growth in holiness] is another reason why the church needs close-knit small groups or covenant cells to undergird its life. Such groups are just as important as the other aids toward spirituality and edification which the church provides," states Howard Snyder.[6]

---

church, or work-related news. Slowly, the group will enter new levels of intimacy. You, small group leader, must skillfully guide the group to these new levels.[7]

> ➤ *Level One:* Small talk (weather, etc.). This is where casual conversation occurs — chitchat. *Example:* How are you today? The weather sure has been cold.
> ➤ *Level Two:* Information or facts. During this level, members of the group exchange facts. *Example:* I just heard today that they're going to raise gas prices even higher.
> ➤ *Level Three:* Ideas and opinions. In this stage, the members feel confident enough to defend ideas, knowing no one's going to discount their input. *Example:* I think the government should set limits on gas prices. If prices keep going up, the economy in general is going to suffer.
> ➤ *Level Four:* Feelings. What's truly happening in our lives. On this level, group members feel confident enough to share feelings. *Example:* I've felt depressed all day, and I'm not sure why.

Level Four group members share their dreams, hopes, fears, and failures. Personal transparency leads to a sense of being known for who we really are. True intimacy lies at this level. Example: "I love to travel, but I struggle with the effect it has on my family. When I came home from my last trip, I noticed my family really needed me. Pray for me this week as I travel to . . ."

The group will enter deeper levels as it grows in maturity. The leader is the key to guiding the group to new levels and must create the atmosphere in which everyone is free to share. When asked open-ended application questions, the group members will talk about what's really on their hearts and minds.

Live Honestly before God and Others

Transparent living begins by meeting daily with God in personal devotions and then honestly communicating with Him throughout the day. Ask God to make you honest and transparent as you spend consistent time in His presence. After living in transparency before God, make it your goal to share your own weaknesses and trials in your daily relationships. Don't feel like you always have to look good before others. Allow God to be

Levels of Communication

➤ **Level One**
Patty: Hi Pauline, How was your trip to California?
Pauline: I enjoyed it a lot.
Patty: What did you do?
Pauline: I mainly spent time visiting family, but I also went a few places with friends.
Patty: Sounds like you had fun.

➤ **Level Two**
Pauline: Yes, I did, but it was also difficult.
Patty: Why?
Pauline: Well, it just seems like there is so much corruption today — in the news, on the streets, just everywhere.

➤ **Level Three**
Patty: I know what you mean. You've probably heard that Ellen — you know the one who is the star of her own TV show — declared herself a lesbian. It made me so angry. I want to learn to love homosexuals, but sometimes I feel so unloving toward them.

➤ **Level Four**
Pauline: For me, lesbianism isn't something I just hear about. I was at one time a lesbian and God rescued me from it five years ago. I still struggle with sexual tendencies toward females, but God gives me strength on a day-to-day basis.

strong in your weaknesses.

My brother Andy's words continue to speak to me today. I certainly haven't arrived. I still have the tendency to impress and hide behind a veneer of strength. Yet as I meditate on God's grace and realize that He's glorified in my weakness, I'm encouraged to live honestly before God and others. Now it's your turn: Are there many entryways in your life?

Points to Remember

Effective small group leaders don't hide behind superficiality, acting like it's unspiritual to experience pain and problems. Rather, they bare their souls through honest transparency. They share deeply, motivating the rest of the group to follow their example. Remember:

Find a Co-mentor

➤ Find one or two close friends with whom you can meet on a regular basis (weekly, bi-weekly, or monthly).

➤ Make it a point to share your weaknesses and trials with this person.

➤ Listen intently to the needs of your friend, while he listens to your needs.

➤ Pray together for the needs expressed.

➤ Close with prayer.

➤ Model transparency in order for the members to do the same.

➤ The Biblical mandate to confess our faults to one another often takes place in the small group meeting.

➤ Aim for transformation rather than simply information.

➤ Guide the group into deeper levels of communication.

➤ Find a mentor who will help you live honestly before God and others.

An Inquisitive Mind

An Inquisitive Mind

The human mind enables small group leaders to think, reflect, and make decisions. Using the mind, a leader can prepare questions that draw out participation and stimulate lively discussion. Well-designed questions turn dry and boring meetings into creative interaction.

Chapter Five

An Inquisitive Mind:
Asking Stimulating Questions

Recently, Peter accepted my challenge to lead four consecutive lessons. Two of them were as dry as a bone, while the others stirred exciting discussion. The difference? Peter's questions. In all four lessons, he listened intently, called individual members by name, and was careful not to dominate. On two occasions, however, he used questions that stimulated participation. Often the difference between effective discussion and the type that fizzles into embarrassed silence has to do with the type of questions the leader asks.

As you train your mind to identify and prepare stimulating, open-ended questions, your small group will soar. The people will leave edified, making plans to return the next week.

Closed Questions Versus Open Questions

During the two sub-par meetings, Peter focused entirely on the Bible passage. We covered the book of Jonah, so Peter asked: "Where did Jonah flee?" "To a ship bound for Tarshish," a member replied. "Great answer," said Peter. "Anyone else?" Silence. "Why did Jonah flee?" asked Peter. "Because he was disobedient," said another member. Peter tried to get more people to talk. "Would anyone else like to share?" A few mumbled a variation of the same answer, but when all was said and done, there was only one answer: Jonah was disobedient.

Peter listened well, gave positive feedback, and did everything right.

What more could the group say? There was basically only one answer to offer. Jonah fled because he was disobedient. Someone might have added a few more adjectives like, "Jonah was gravely disobedient," but why bother? Even a superb, highly trained leader couldn't elicit more discussion from the question. Peter could have waited in silence for an hour, hoping for someone else to talk, and we'd have sat there in silence with him.

I talked to Peter a few days later. I shared with him my own failures and discoveries — especially in the area of asking questions.

Something clicked in Peter and the next lesson was excellent. We covered Psalm 46:1, "God is our refuge and strength, an ever-present help in trouble." Peter began with a few closed, observation questions to help us understand the Biblical text. But this time he quickly applied the Biblical passage to our own lives, with questions like, "When was the last time you had a crisis? How did you handle it?" Peter followed with another application question, "How did God become a refuge in your life through your crisis?"

Everyone had something to share. "Many years ago I administered the most successful tailoring business in the country," Paul began. "I loved my job and even made suits for the president. At the height of my success, the doctors told me it was either my health or my job, so I had to leave it. But God . . ."

Then Carol shared, "Recently, my daughter Mary said she'd be home at 10 P.M., but at 1 A.M. she still hadn't arrived. I'm a nervous person anyway, but this time I was beyond myself. Through prayer God began . . ." Our group shared deeply that night. We bore each other's burdens. We went away edified, encouraged, and eager to come back for more.

Preparing the right questions before you start the meeting can give you assurance that the discussion will be lively and dynamic. Closed questions have only one correct answer. When a leader uses too many of them, he positions himself as a Bible expert who's trying to discover the brightest, most Biblically literate students.

Open-ended questions, on the other hand, elicit discussion and sharing. There is more than one right answer. Open-ended questions stir small group members to apply Biblical truths to their own lives.

Questions **Not** to Ask[1]

➤ **The "machine gun" question**
Question: Give three reasons Jesus asked the apostles who they thought He was, and tell me how you would answer His question.
Problems: It asks more than one question, yet sounds like it's looking for a specific answer. Notice that it's not concise or contestable. When a question gets too complex with sub-parts and various clauses, participants tend to get confused.

➤ **The "over-your-head" question**
Question: What are the theological implications of Peter's acclamation with regard to Trinitarian versus Unitarian doctrines, and what does that imply about the ontological argument?
Problems: This is over the heads of all but the Bible-college professors in your group. (Not clear and coherent, concise or creative. May also be inconsiderate.) You might not ask a question this ridiculous, but be careful of asking questions you understand but are still beyond the understanding of most of your group.

➤ **The "what-did-you-say?" question**
Question: How did you feel when you repeated the good confession?
Problems: Definitely not considerate, and perhaps not complete. Have all your members repeated the good confession? If yours is a new group, is this too personal, too fast?

➤ **The "exam" question**
Question: What three attitudes was Jesus looking for when he asked this question?
Problems: This isn't a discussion question; it's a test. It's looking for one "correct" answer (actually three). It also is not complete. How would anyone know what attitudes Jesus was looking for?

➤ **The "ozone" question**
Question: What was going through the apostle John's mind as Peter answered Jesus' question?
Problems: How can anyone really know? It's incomplete and not very challenging. You could possibly rephrase this question by saying, "If you were the apostle John, what would be going through your mind?"

Preparing Dynamic Questions

Let's look at an example from the familiar passage in John 3:16: "For God so loved the world that he gave his one and only Son, that whoever believes in him shall not perish but have eternal life."

Observation

You could start out with a closed-ended *observation* question: "How did God demonstrate his love for us?" The answer lies within the text. In this case, you're simply asking the people to *observe* and answer what they see in the verse. Even a Hindu who had never read the Bible could answer the question: "God demonstrated his love by sending His Son."

It's great to include a few observation questions in the beginning of the small group lesson. Such questions will help your members understand the meaning of the Bible passage.

Interpretation

You could go one step further and ask your small group members to interpret what the verse means, yet for the most part this is still a closed question. For example, you could ask: "What kind of love did God demonstrate?" Some might talk about God's sacrificial love; others might refer to God's Fatherly compassion.

The leader might be ready to talk about the Greek word *agape*, which refers to Christ's self-sacrificing love on the cross. While there is room for a few such *interpretation* questions to better understand the Bible, this is not the goal of the small group. If you use this type of question too frequently, your members will leave with lots of knowledge but little transformation in their own lives.

Observation and interpretation questions help us understand the Bible, but for the most part they're closed questions. They reach the head but not the heart. They can provide useful Biblical information, but they'll generate little interaction.

Application

Let's look at an open-ended application question covering John 3:16. You could say: "Describe your experience when you first understood that God loves you." You could then call on one of the believers in the group: "Susan, would you share what happened when you first experienced God's love for you?"

This type of question/exhortation takes the well-known verse in John and invites members to apply it. Many will share. You could also ask a question like: "How did you come to know God loves you? Did someone talk to you about God? Were you alone in your room? Share your experience."

Grab the Heart

Several years ago, I visited a small group that was discussing the parable of the unmerciful servant in Matthew 18:21-35. The small group leader asked question after question about what the text said (observation), then a few more questions about what the text meant (interpretation), but not once did he ask the people to apply these verses to their own lives. He missed a perfect opportunity. He could have said: "Share an experience when you felt bitterness toward another person." He could have followed with: "Share how you overcame those feelings and were able to forgive that

Practice Drill

Philippians 4:13: "I can do everything through him who gives me strength."

➤ *Observation question:* "How many things can we do through Christ's strength?"
➤ *Interpretation question:* "Why does this verse only apply to believers?"
➤ *Application question:* "How has Christ given you strength in this past week?"

Questions that Grab the Heart

➤ *Examples of questions that generate discussion:*
  • Share your experience concerning . . .
  • What is God saying to you right now from this passage?
  • How will you apply this passage during the week?

➤ *Example of closed questions that elicit one answer:*
  • What does this passage say about . . .
  • Do you agree with this passage?

person." Most likely there were people that very night who needed freedom from pent-up bitterness and who were longing to share with others.

Questions Worth Repeating²

Questions should focus on the main meaning of the passage and its application. Here are four questions that can be used repeatedly with some variation:

➤ What stands out to you in this passage?
➤ What seems to be the main point of this passage?
➤ Can you illustrate this truth from an experience in your life?
➤ What is God saying to you right now?

Make sure you grab the heart during the small group lesson. Don't allow your members to leave the group without having applied the Bible to their own lives. I know of one small group leader who concludes the Word time by saying: "In light of what we've read and discussed in this passage, how do you think God wants to use this in your life or the life of this group?"

I recommend, as a minimum, one application question for every two observation/interpretation questions.

Christian A. Schwarz and his team from the Institute for Church Development in Germany have proven that direct application to immediate needs makes the difference between an effective and ineffective small group. They analyzed responses from 4.2 million people, from more than 1,000 churches in 32 countries. Schwarz concluded that successful small groups must be ". . . holistic small groups which go beyond just discussing Bible passages to applying its message to daily life." In these groups, members are able to bring up those issues and questions that are immediate personal concerns.³

Aim at Transformation

Every lesson should give people something to feel, to remember, and to do. The goal of the small group is to transform lives, rather than take in knowledge. For this reason, it's great to remind small group members about last week's challenge and determine if anything significant happened.

The leader might start the lesson time by saying, "You'll remember that last week we discussed 1 John 3:16-17. Let me read these verses again: "This is how we know what love is: Jesus Christ laid down his life for us. And we ought to lay down our lives for our brothers. If anyone has material possessions and sees his brother in need but has no pity on him, how can the love of God be in him?" Then ask, "Can anyone give a testimony about performing an act of kindness for someone during the past week?"

Just wait in silence for a few moments. If no one shares, at least they'll know you're expecting transformation from the small group lesson, rather than mere Bible knowledge. If you begin the lesson each week by asking how people acted on the previous lesson, the members will begin to look for ways to apply the lesson. This calls for vulnerability in your own life as well. If you failed to act on last week's lesson, admit it. People will appreciate your honesty.

Apply as You Go

Some lessons have 5-10 closed-ended questions and then end with a section called "application." It's far better to apply as you go. Start with an observation question that helps to understand the biblical passage. Then ask an application question like, "What is God saying to you right now from this passage?" Another great application question is, "How will you apply these truths during the following week?"

Explain the Passage Clearly

Although the lesson is based on questions, the members must understand the general context of the Bible passage in order to answer them.

Don't sit in silence for an hour, waiting for a response! If group members don't understand the question, their puzzled faces will reveal it. Perhaps the confusion occurred because they don't understand the Biblical context. In the minds of the hearers, the question appears in thin air with no concrete base.

I recommend, therefore, that the leader initiate the small group lesson (the Word time) with a question about the biblical passage. A great observation question to begin with is, "What does this passage say?" Everyone can share what the text says while the leader gives a brief explanation of the passage.

There's no excuse for sloppy, superficial Bible study. Some leaders erroneously think participatory question-based lessons don't require as much preparation time as monologue Bible studies. Wrong!

Limit Your Questions

One of the most common errors in small group agendas is including too many discussion questions. Some small group leaders feel obligated to cover all the questions — even if there are ten or more.

A good Word time has three to five questions. If small group leaders try to cover more than that, the extroverts in the group will dominate the meeting.

My advice is to allow the people to leave with a hunger for more, rather than a commitment never to return to such a long, boring small group meeting. I also think it's important to leave time for prayer after the small group lesson. It's best to reach a crescendo of deep sharing that naturally leads to deep praying.

What's a Huddle Meeting?

A huddle meeting is a leadership meeting between small group leader and his or her coach. It could be a one-on-one time between coach and small group leader or a group time between coach and all five small group leaders. Some coaches care for as many as twelve small group leaders, but I recommend caring for three.[4]

Written Assignments and Newcomers

Some small groups follow a study guide or book that each member is required to buy, study during the week, and bring to each small group meeting.

I don't recommend this practice for ongoing, open small group groups. The main reason is a practical one. How would you feel if you showed up at a meeting for the first time and everyone but you had answers to the leader's questions already written out? Intimidated? Certainly, and most likely you'd never return (especially if the group was in the middle of the book of Revelation!).

The perfect place for written study guides is a huddle meeting between small group leaders and coaches. The small group, however, must always give the benefit of the doubt to the person who enters the group for the first time.

It's the Question!

It's the question, small group leader. Just maybe, the lack of participation in your small group is the result of too many closed-ended questions rather than your skills as a small group leader. Before becoming too discouraged, thinking you lack communication skills, examine the types of questions you've been using. Begin to make sure you include open-ended application questions toward the beginning of your small group lesson, and watch your small group come to life.

Points to Remember

Successful small group leaders use their minds to create stimulating application questions that promote participation. They realize the wording of the question often makes the difference between success and failure. Remember:

> ➤ Open questions are preferable to closed questions.
> ➤ Apply the Bible through application questions.
> ➤ Aim at transformation rather than information.
> ➤ Explain the passage clearly in order to apply it.
> ➤ Limit the number of questions.

Listening Ears

Listening Ears

Great small group leaders prioritize listening to others, knowing that everyone has a story that needs to be heard. God has given us two ears and only one mouth for a reason. The small group environment is perfectly suited for active listening to occur.

Chapter Six

Listening Ears

President Theodore Roosevelt, known as a man of action, was a great listener. He expected this quality in other people. Once, at a gala ball, he grew tired of meeting people who returned his remarks with stiff, mindless pleasantries. So he began to greet people with a smile, saying, "Murdered my grandmother this morning." Most people, so nervous about meeting him, didn't even hear what he said. But one diplomat did. Upon hearing the president's remark, he leaned over and whispered to him, "I'm sure she had it coming to her!"

Fine-tuned, listening ears are a rare commodity. It's far easier to partially listen, while wandering off into our own dreams and plans. I believe, that listening, more than talking, distinguishes effective communicators from the rest.

Most of us are so filled with our autobiography that we really don't attempt to understand another person's point of view. We first want others to understand us. Great listeners seek *first to understand.*

Facilitative Speaking

Facilitative speaking involves the use of questions and suggestions to encourage further exploration: "John, I hear you saying you need to communicate more in your marriage. All of us here tonight can relate to this. John, how do you think you could start improving your communication?"

The Member's Response Takes Priority

"The customer is always right" is the mantra for a growing number of successful companies. In the small group, the *needs of the members* guide exciting lesson times.

What you have to say, leader, is not as important as the thoughts of those present! Focus on them, not on yourself, and everyone will leave edified. The best gift you can give your members is to listen intently.

When the leader has listened intently to the answer, the group will know it. A sense of satisfaction will fill the room. Perhaps a moment of silence will settle on the group. That's okay. You don't need to say anything in particular because the fruit of listening well will present itself. The next point in the discussion flows naturally.

Why It's So Difficult to Listen

One reason is that the average person speaks at approximately 125 to 150 words per minute while listeners can easily process some 500 words per minute. Because of this "lag time," it's easy to nod, smile and act like you're listening, while thinking about something else.

Listen Actively

Active listening is vigorous, energetic, and diligent. It requires listening to every word, like a heat-seeking missile homing in on an enemy aircraft. It takes hard work and effort to think about someone else's interest more than your own.

Most of us are accustomed to pseudo-listening. We nod our head, as if we're listening, while our thoughts might be in another, altogether different meeting. It's tempting to think about the next question, the ringing telephone, or the hassles at work.

Great leaders listen to every word a person says . . . to the very end. I know it's hard, but when your small group members recognize your active listening skills, they'll follow your example.

A Bad Habit

"Most people do not listen to understand; they listen in order to answer. While the other is talking, they are preparing their reply," says Stephen Covey.[1]

Listen to What is *Not* Said

The science of kinesics — or *body language* — is the study of nonverbal communication.[2] Since 60 percent of all communication involves body language, it's important to listen to what is *not* said.

Gestures, such as a bored look, an incredulous stare, or a humorous glance to a friend express what a person is actually thinking.[3]

I've witnessed hurried small group leaders demonstrate their distraction when someone's responding. It might be a gesture, a look at their watch, or a quick look at the next question. But the non-verbal message rings loud and clear: what you're sharing is unimportant, wrong, or inappropriate. The leader's own responsiveness through actions and gestures will set the tone of the small group meetings.

A wise leader might say, "Linda, you look like you're thinking about something. Do you have something to add?" "Well, now that you mention it, I did want to say something."

Non-Verbal Check for Small Group Leaders

When someone answers a question, do you normally respond with:
➤ A smile?
➤ A nod of the head?
➤ An offer to help?

Or, unconsciously, do you:
➤ Have a scowl on your face
➤ Show little responsiveness
➤ Delay acting upon the needs of those present

Non-verbal Listening

➤ ***Tip one:*** Be transparent. If you're tired, have had a bad day, or are wrestling with something, just let the group know. Your transparency will stimulate others to freely share as well. Otherwise, your small group members might think you're angry with them. The small group is the time to share reality and not to hide.

➤ ***Tip two:*** Be filled with the Spirit. Leaders who are filled with Christ are far more effective in responding — both verbally and non-verbally — to small group members. Jesus Christ provides the missing link.

Non-Verbal Listening

To stimulate conversation by participants:

➤ Keep an open body position (do not cross your arms or legs toward the group).

➤ Lean forward to show interest.

➤ Nod and smile to show agreement.

➤ Make brief eye contact to encourage conversation from a quiet person.

How did this small group leader know Linda wanted to say something? He observed her sitting on the edge of her chair, rubbing her chin, tapping her foot. He read her body language.[4]

Listen to Your Members Concerning Your Leadership

Whenever I teach a seminar or course, I ask the participants to evaluate my ministry. Often I have to force myself to read the evaluations, because I don't like to receive criticism. But I know I'll never get better unless I know how to improve. Evaluations point out weak areas and highlight strong ones.[5]

One chapter in Tom Peters' book, *Thriving On Chaos*, is called "Become Obsessed With Listening." He writes, "With most competitors moving ever faster, the race will go to those who listen (and respond) most intently."[6] Small group leaders listen in order to improve the quality of the group. And the consequences of listening are far more than inheriting earthly possessions. Eternal treasures are at stake.

I'd advise you to ask your small group members how you can improve your leadership. Ask them if their needs are being met in the small group. Ask them if there's something you can do to improve the group atmosphere. Listen to them.

Listening through Repetition

I've learned the power of clarifying and restating what group members say. One night we were discussing 1 Timothy 4:12, "Don't let anyone look down on you because you are young, but set an example for the believers . . ." After a few observation questions, I asked, "Can you share about a time when your example influenced someone else?"

Christina started, "In high school, my friends mockingly named me "pastor." Yet, as time passed, they came to me for counsel and soon I began a small group on campus with those same name-callers."

I responded, "Your example attracted those who mocked you and you were able to counsel them and minister to them. Great example! Others?" This practice has many advantages. Here are a few:

➤ It gives the person a chance to say, "No, I really didn't mean that. Here's what I meant . . ." Communication is a difficult process, full of hazards and potential pitfalls. We think we understand what the person is saying, but often our own biases and experience cloud the true meaning. Restating the person's idea in your own words will help you avoid misunderstanding and enrich the Bible discussion.

➤ Restating the idea will give hesitant folks more time to formulate a response. If you're covering Romans 12: 17-21, you might say, "Thanks, Joe, for that response. How true that we should repay good for evil. But as you said, we often forget we've surrendered our rights to Jesus Christ."

➤ It will make the leader a better listener. Many signals seem to cross the leader's mind when someone is talking (e.g., the next question, the atmosphere of the home, gestures, personal worries, etc.). The discipline of restating the member's words will help the leader focus on listening.

Learn from the Business World

The effective professional salesman doesn't speak until he understands the customers needs. He seeks to understand (what does my customer need) while the amateur wants to be understood (I have the best product). Stephen Covey says, ". . . an effective sales person first seeks to understand the needs of the customer. The amateur sells products; the professional sells solutions to the needs of the customer."[7]

➤ Restating the comment demonstrates love to the person. It shouts loudly that the leader has taken the response seriously. When the leader quickly darts to the next question, just the opposite message is communicated.

➤ It helps those in the group who have *not* been actively listening to understand the person's comments. When someone else is speaking, it's easy for other members to revert back to their own problems and questions. Restating the idea will help everyone stay on the same page.

Refuse to Answer Your Own Questions

"What does verse four tell us?" John asked the group. Silence. "Does anyone want to share with the group what verse four means?" More silence. "Well, let me share with you what it means . . ." Facilitators quickly convert into preachers at the first signs of silence.

When you ask a question, you've placed the ball in the court of the members, and now expect them to reply. When the small group leader embarks on an impromptu sermon, small group members feel cheated. "I thought he wanted me to share," a member inwardly fumes. "Why does he dominate so much?" another thinks. Many small group leaders feel insecure while waiting for a reply.

When you answer your own questions, you communicate that an answer isn't expected. They'll think, "He's only baiting us with an initial question, but he really wants to answer it himself." People will even stop responding altogether.

The leader has already spent lots of time meditating on the questions, studying the passage, and looking at the different angles. The small group member has just heard the question for the first time. Many thoughts are bombarding the member's mind:

➤ "What does the Bible passage really mean?"
➤ "How should I answer this question?"
➤ "My answer is too obvious."
➤ "I'd prefer if someone else spoke first."
➤ "Maybe I should wait for the next question."
➤ "I've already talked too much."
➤ "I don't think I have the right answer."

Then finally, the light turns on, "That's it, I have it, I think I'll share."

The first few seconds after launching the question is a time of digestion. Give the members time to chew on the question.

While the small group member is rehearsing the response, the small group leader might be anxiously thinking:

➤ "Was this a good question?"
➤ "Did I express the question correctly?"
➤ "Why isn't anyone responding?"
➤ "Should I call on someone?"
➤ "I wish there was more participation!"

Don't be Afraid of Silence

Learn to expect lulls in the small group meeting. Frequently, when it seems like nothing is happening, God is working in a powerful way. Since the small group is more of an encounter than a performance, the small group leader should not be alarmed at times of quietness in the meeting.

When someone does finally share, the small group leader feels relieved. Relax! Give your people time to think and respond. Ralph Neighbour offers this wise counsel:

> I learned years ago to briefly introduce the topic to the group and then stare at the toe of my shoe. By doing so, I was indicating that I would no longer control what happens. After a period of silence, someone invariably speaks. He or she probably addresses me as they do so, but I deliberately do not establish eye contact. The group realizes that I have released them and will not guide the discussion. In that freedom, the body members begin to listen for the voice of the Head, Jesus, instead of the voice of the facilitator. What happens next can be awesome![8]

Ask for Additional Responses

One response per question is a poor ratio. Wise small group leaders want more; they ask the members of the group for additional responses. Some small group members are introverted and must gather courage to break through their own sound barrier in order to say something.[9]

Listen Empathetically before Advising

Often people come to a small group to receive healing. They're filled with pent-up emotions and hurts: wounds from careless criticism or judgment; rejection in childhood; a failing marriage. Some have been hurt time and time again and are looking to the small group for some type of affirmation. They need close community where they can grow, receive care, and slowly heal.

At some point, the person might find the courage to *really share* with the group (level four communication). This type of openness requires guts. Those who step out on a limb to share transparently must know the limb won't be cut down. The group's response will stimulate either healing or rejection.

Most people intellectually understand their problems. Why do they share them? Because they're looking for a listening ear, a chance to be heard. Instead of listening and empathizing with the person, certain

Listening and Giving Advice

When a group member begins to share burdens he or she needs the group to bear, the group should be more ready to listen than do anything else (James 1:19). Often the person sharing doesn't want advice or counsel but just an understanding ear.

➤ *Helpful listening responses:*
- Paraphrasing (restating in your own words what you heard the person say).
- Short affirmations ending in ways that open the door for the other to share more.

➤ *Unhelpful listening responses*
- Reassuring them that they don't have much of a problem (this implies that you disagree with their judgment that they have a problem, which makes them stop talking).
- Sending quick advice (we don't know the situation).

➤ *How to tell if others want your ear or your advice:*
- Watch their body language when you send advice.
- Keep your responses short, letting them choose what to talk about. Do they continue to unload their troubles, change the subject, or pursue your counsel?

leaders have the tendency to hop on Biblical horses and plunge spears into the person. After all, isn't God holy and doesn't He hate sin? Yes, but we're not God! Remember the compassion He's had on us. We must do likewise.

When someone is facing a crisis, it's not the moment to say, "You just need to trust in the Lord. Don't you know that all things work together for good to those who love God, to those who are called according to His purpose?" This advice, while 100 percent correct, will do more harm than good to a hurting, grieving person. Before advice, the person first must know that God's people will help bear the burden. He or she is longing for a listening ear — not a quick Biblical response.

Roberta Hestenes says, "Far too often, group members are quick to offer advice to problems instead of carefully listening. This type of advice-giving often does more harm than good."[10]

Example of Effective Empathy

When our second baby was stillborn in 1992, a friend named George approached me one day and simply placed his hand on my shoulder as we waited a few moments in silence. Without saying a word, he ministered more to me than anyone else in that difficult time period. In small group ministry, when someone unburdens his or her soul, it's the time for the rest of the group to bear that burden and to communicate sympathy, rather than memorized Bible verses. One of the best healing tools is just to listen.

I believe that there needs to be a moment of silent understanding, when a burden is accepted and shared. As the members empathize with the person, godly counsel will ensue: "Joan, I can relate to your fears and doubts brought on by your friend's cancer. When my brother faced brain cancer, I felt those same fears. I wrestled for days, wondering why God would allow it. But then God showed me . . ." The scales of past wounds will peel away and the new creature in Christ will appear as the small group ministers through empathetic listening.

Small group leader, advise your group to listen, rather than quickly responding with pat answers. Demonstrate what you want them to do by your actions. People won't follow what you say; they'll follow what you do. Preparing a healing community may take some time, but it's worth the wait.

How to Treat People

Viktor Frankl said, "If you treat people to a vision of themselves . . . you make them become what they are capable of becoming."[11]

The Essence of Listening: Others

Paul advised the church in Philippi, "Do nothing out of selfish ambition or vain conceit, but in humility consider others better than yourselves. Each of you should look not only to your own interests, but also to the interests of others" (Philippians 2:3-4). He then added, "I hope in the Lord Jesus to send Timothy to you soon, that I also may be cheered when I receive news about you. I have no one else like him, who takes a genuine interest in your welfare. For everyone looks out for his own interests, not those of Jesus Christ." Paul rejoiced in sending Timothy to the church because he would truly focus on the needs of those present (Philippians 2:19-21).

This anonymous quote clarifies the leader's job: "Others, Lord, yes others, may this my motto be, help me to live for others, that I might be like thee."[12]

Points to Remember

Active listening allows a small group leader to express love in a practical way. When small group members know the leader is a good listener, they'll share more freely and consistently. Remember:

➤ The member's response takes priority over your own.
➤ Practice active listening (truly hearing what the person is saying).
➤ Listen to what is not said (gestures, etc.).
➤ Listen to feedback from the members about your leadership.
➤ Refuse to answer your own questions.
➤ Ask the group for additional responses after one person has shared.
➤ Limit advice giving in the group (instead, practice empathetic listening).

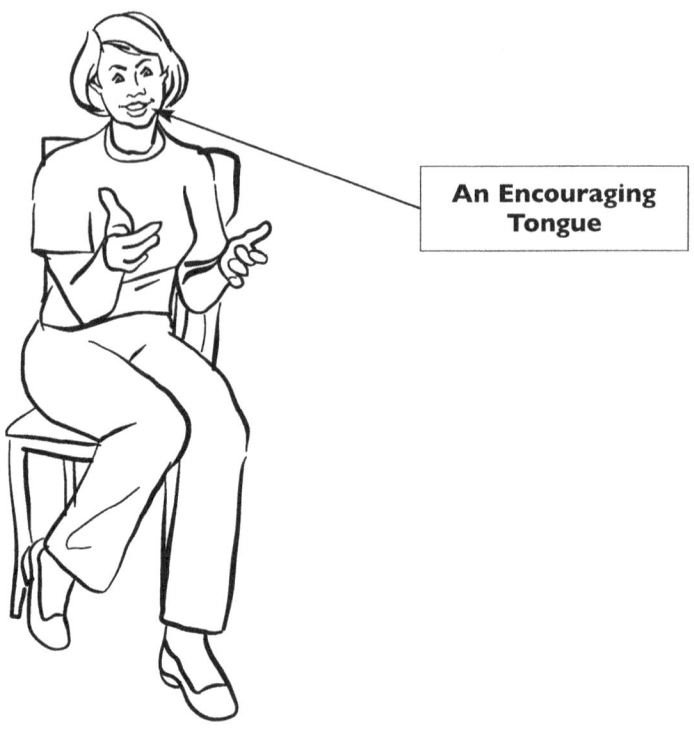

An Encouraging
Tongue

An Encouraging Tongue

The tongue can encourage, discourage, or even destroy. A small group leader must choose words that encourage. Proverbs says: "From the fruit of his mouth a man's stomach is filled; with the harvest from his lips he is satisfied" (18:20).

Chapter Seven

An Encouraging Tongue

It's no accident that the words "community," "communion," and "communication" all sound alike. These words share common roots from the Latin words for *with* and *one*. They involve being *with one another* and being *one with each other*. It's all about communication that leads to communion. Small groups enable regular church members to communicate God's Word and apply it to their own lives, thus growing in community with God and others.

Small group leaders edify with their mouths, thus creating an atmosphere of communion. Their goal is to build-up, edify, and, in the process, transform their hearers.

A good friend of mine once said to me, "I've seen so many meetings that have been correctly led from a technical point of view, which lack any power because the people do not have any relationship." Is it possible to know all about how to listen, ask questions, facilitate, share transparently, and still fail in the small group? I believe so. The goal of communication is community — not technical perfection.

Influence

"The length and breadth of our influence upon others depends upon the depth of our concern for others."

Great Communication Encourages

I'll never forget the meeting in which one small group leader offered a slight criticism to every response given. "You almost have it," James said. Another person responded to the answer and James retorted, "No, that's not it, but you're getting closer." The dance to find the right answer continued. "This is like a high school quiz," I thought to myself. As James reached the last few questions, the participation ground to a screeching halt. No one wanted to risk embarrassment.

You can always find something good in each reply. The fact that the member dared to speak is positive. Give the person credit at every opportunity. Affirm the idea-giver, even if you can't fully endorse the idea. Thank the person for the comment, regardless of whether it is right or wrong.

UCLA basketball coach John Wooden told players who scored to smile, wink, or nod to the player who passed them the ball. "What if he's not looking?" asked a team member. Wooden replied, "I guarantee he'll look." Everyone values encouragement and looks for it — especially when the leader is a consistent encourager.

Never Totally Reject an Idea

Never totally reject any idea. Find a way to explore the good in the idea. Affirm the person who gave the idea, even though you're not in full agreement with it.

Three Right Ways to Respond to a Wrong Answer

➤ Take the blame for miscommunication: "I guess I didn't state that question very clearly — what I'm really asking is . . .
➤ Give an example: Here's an illustration of what I mean . . .
➤ Allow others in the group to give the right answers: "Ummmm. What do the rest of you think?"

Dealing with the Talker

The small group offers a warm environment in which open sharing thrives. This is extremely positive but danger lurks as well. Some people gravitate to small groups in order to

If a Person Gives a Doctrinally Incorrect Answer...

Even if an answer is not based on Scripture (off doctrine), thank the person for the response and read the passage in Scripture that reveals the truth. Or say, "Thanks for your response. I'm going to do some more study on this topic. I'd like to share my findings next week."

express their opinions, however negative and combative they may be. They take advantage of the warm atmosphere to unload on others, to find a vent for their insecurity. These people love to hear their own voices. Their own insights, they think, far exceed anyone else's. No one has an opportunity to contribute while they are talking, and group members will come to resent their comments and behaviors.

Dealing with talkers is probably the greatest challenge in small group meetings. I've said repeatedly that small group leaders shouldn't dominate the group. This also means, however, that one or two group members must not dominate.

The small group leader is the gatekeeper, the protector of the flock, and must realize that if he permits one person to dominate the meeting, the freedom of expression of individual members will suffer.

Since I've been leading my current small group, I've had to deal with at least three dedicated talkers. I've struggled with each one and constantly had to stay on top of the situation. I've often wavered between two competing emotions. When I've tried to use extra love, I've felt trampled on. Yet, when I've sought to control the talker, I've felt unloving and uneasy.

Talkers

"Excessive talkers will drain the life of a group."[1]

Here are some practical steps to overcome this problem:

> ➤ Sit next to the talker in order to give them less eye contact. Talkers don't need lots of encouragement. They might even feel that you, the leader, are encouraging their nonstop conversation

by eye contact, nods, and a listening ear. Sitting next to the person and avoiding eye contact will signal that you're not encouraging him or her.

➤ Call on other people to give their opinions. When you call on a person by name, you're saying to the rest: *"Wait your turn."* For example, Jim has been dominating the conversation for the last two questions during the lesson time. For the next question, call on Judy to give the answer. When she's finished, call on Mark for an additional reply. By calling on individuals by name, you're assuming leadership responsibility and directing the conversation of the group.

➤ Redirect the conversation away from the talker, if he or she pauses. Granted, this is a more drastic measure. When I share this tactic at a small group seminar, the crowd roars with laughter. They can just picture the small group leader waiting for the talker to take a deep breath (preparing for another Bible homily) to give someone else a chance. Although hilarious, it depicts something very serious — one person dominating the group discussion. Leaders must shield the small group from such control.

➤ Talk directly with the person. Often, talkers simply don't understand the purpose of a small group. They sincerely think others need their constant input and spiritual wisdom. They've never realized the purpose of the small group is to allow everyone to participate and share. Talking directly with the person, before or after the small group meeting will often solve the problem.

➤ If the problem persists, talk to the person directly over you (e.g., coach, pastor, elder, etc.). Most likely that leader has more

Christ and Confrontation

Christ taught us the Father's plan of going to the person personally when he said, "If your brother sins against you, go and show him his fault, just between the two of you. If he listens to you, you have won your brother over" (Mt. 18: 15). When going personally to the talker, explain the importance of participation in the group.

experience in dealing with such issues and can offer valuable insight to resolve the conflict.

➤ Ask the person to help you make the meeting more participatory. I gave a small group seminar in New Jersey and afterwards a successful small group leader approached me saying, "I've found a great way to deal with the constant talker that works every time." He continued, "Ask the talker to help you get others talking." This advice makes sense. When the talker understands the larger reason for the small group and even how to participate in fulfilling this goal, it's likely the person will change.

➤ Clarify the rule that no one is allowed to speak a second time until everyone has had a chance to speak for the first time. Such an exhortation works better in a mature group. If you have many non-Christians in your group, you need to use discernment. Explain that the purpose of this rule is to liberate the silent ones to participate more. It will also remind the talkers in a clear, concrete way to remain quiet until others have shared.[2]

Keeping the Communication Lines Open

Connie Conflict and Annie Anger are neighbors. They hate one another. No one is quite sure when the animosity began, although there are lots of stories. Each of them joined the group without knowing the other was there.[3] Now there's open warfare! Each has steadfastly declared she won't leave and let the other win. What can you do?

The Apostle Paul faced conflict in the churches he started. He exhorted two people in the church in Philippi to make peace with each other, "I plead with Euodia and I plead with Syntyche to agree with each other in the Lord"(Phil. 4:2). For whatever

Dealing with Conflicts

Every family fights. The issue is, do they fight righteously? Withdrawal isn't an option. Nor is gossip or backbiting. The only way out is to calmly approach those who offend you, ask good questions to establish their actions and motives, and give or receive forgiveness as the situation demands. If you get stuck, get someone else to help you through.

Potential Areas of Conflict

Why do conflicts exist in small groups?

➤ Each person arrives with a different set of expectations. One might expect in-depth Bible study, mountain-top worship, spiritual warfare, analytical counseling, a charismatic believer's session, or an evangelistic campaign. When individual expectations are not met, conflict ensues.

➤ Certain personalities do not mix well. Just because a person is a Christian doesn't mean he or she will always mesh well with other believers.

➤ People in the group participate in different ways. Quiet and dominant group members participate so differently that conflict might arise.

➤ Some small group members might not agree with the leadership style of the one leading the group. Perhaps they're more domineering, decisive, or democratic, while tending to judge those leaders who lead differently.

reason, they were causing dissension in the house church in Philippi. Matthew Henry points out,

"Sometimes there is need of applying the general precepts of the gospel to particular persons and cases. Euodia and Syntyche, it seems, were at variance, either one with the other or with the church; either upon a civil account (it may be they were engaged in a lawsuit) or upon a religious account — it may be they were of different opinions and sentiments."[4]

Most of us live by the maxim, "Avoid conflict at all costs." But conflict and disagreement will happen no matter what you do or how well you do it. A Chinese proverb declares, "The diamond cannot be polished without friction, nor the man perfected without trials." Imagine a small group with a sign on the front door, "Conflict is Expected and Welcome!" Most of us would panic when we saw that sign, but, in reality, a small group often runs more like a hospital than a country club.

Conflict can lead to improved conditions and growth. It can reveal the group's hidden values and assumptions that need to be examined. When people in the group know they can express both positive and negative feelings, their group experience will be genuine. New levels of understanding will flow as the group irons out differences. Fisher and Ellis paraphrase, "The group that fights together stays together."[5]

What's the best way to deal with people in conflict? First, recognize the problem. Hiding it under a bush will only increase doubt among the members. Everyone knows it's there, so why hide it? You might say to an angry member, "I sense you're upset. We need to deal with this difference of opinion." Conflict can't be dealt with until it's recognized and brought into the open.

An example of an opening statement might be,

> It seems to me that you are both feeling quite upset about your differences on this issue. I hear you both stating your position with passionate conviction, but I'm not sure that you're really listening to each other because I hear no one stopping to paraphrase or acknowledge common ground. I'd like to suggest that we back up for a moment and clarify where you agree and disagree with each other. Are you willing to do that?[6]

Second, pray. You won't solve the conflict without concerted prayer. You need to pray for wisdom and discernment.

Third, talk privately to each offending party. If both persons decide to stay in the group (and that's unlikely in the long run), you can't allow their argument to polarize the group or create an uncomfortable environment. You need to talk with each of them separately and be very clear about the ground rules. If the feud continues, treat them as unrepentant individuals continuing in sin.

If the issue is between you and someone in your group, it's best to confront the person using the Lord's own pattern: "If your brother sins against you, go and show him his fault, just between the two of you. If he listens to you, you have won your brother over" (Mt. 18:15). As the leader, if you notice conflict between two members, encourage them to talk privately to each other. Unresolved conflicts are liabilities. Few things undermine a group faster than several members frustrated with one another or a leader who is frustrated with a member.

Fourth, get people to listen to each other. Research in communication has repeatedly found a tendency among conflicting parties to distort or omit information during times of heated disagreement. You can help solve this by asking them to engage in active listening, with empathy for the other person's unique experiences

85

and situation. Help them to criticize ideas, not people. Achieve understanding of all points of view. Deal with all emotions and feelings.

Fifth, include only those who are immediately affected. Some disagreements don't need to see the light of day in a group; deal "off-line" with the person or persons concerned. Admittedly, there are times when the entire group should be involved in problem solving. But try to keep it controlled and resolution-focused, with only those people who need to be restored in relationship.

Communication Without Walls

Don't take the difference of opinion in the group as an attack on your leadership or personality. Separate yourself from the thought. By welcoming the difference of opinion, you'll sharpen your own understanding. When others in the group have differing opinions, view this as an honest opportunity to understand another point of view, not as a threat to authority.

I've been impressed with how my good friend René Naranjo embraces the different opinions in his group. He knows non-Christians need space before coming to Jesus. They need to feel accepted, even with their opposing point of view. Through unconditional love and acceptance, he has seen dozens of non-Christians slowly accept Jesus. Doubters in his group are often melted by the love of Jesus as they continue to attend meetings.

Use different viewpoints to expand the topic. Take advantage of diverse perspectives to expand the discussion and be thankful people are talking.

Remember that effective communication leads to communion. As your small group learns to communicate more effectively — despite conflict — you'll grow in community with God and others.

Communication Tips That Build Community

The writer of Hebrews says, "And let us consider how we may spur one another on toward love and good deeds. Let us not give up meeting together, as some are in the habit of doing, but *let us encourage one another* — and all the more as you see the Day approaching" (Hebrews 10: 24-25). Some of the best ways to spur others on to love and good deeds are:

➤ Show that you care from the moment someone walks in the door. A smile or a hug is the best. When I visited Tony's small group, I arrived before anyone else. Tony met me at the door, gave me a big hug, offered me some refreshment, and politely excused himself for a few moments. I felt welcomed. Tony could have looked at his watch, given me a worried look, and pointed me to a seat as he took care of his responsibilities. Instead, he made me feel welcome. He demonstrated genuine care and concern.

➤ Respond enthusiastically to people throughout the meeting (during the lesson, worship, prayer, icebreaker, and vision casting). Remember that enthusiasm is not just reserved for people with "bubbly" personalities. It's possible to have a melancholic personality and demonstrate enthusiasm.

➤ Pray for your small group members during the week (if possible, do it daily) and then tell them you've been praying for them. They can't hear this enough. People feel protected and loved when they know their small group leader has been praying for them.

➤ Ask questions about their personal lives. Normally the best time to do this is immediately before or after the meeting. Ask them about their family, work, dreams, and visions. On Sunday, when you see them at church, make it a point to greet them and care for them. Without even knowing it, you're fulfilling the role of a pastor by caring for your sheep.

➤ Be aware of any physical needs and seek to meet them. My wife and I were probably the only ones in our church who knew Paul and Elizabeth were hurting physically. During the prayer time in our small group, they shared their personal needs, and we came face to face with their desperate condition. We felt led by God to help them financially, further cementing our relationship with them.

➤ Share part of your own life with them. I love computers and computer-related activity. I brought one of my small group members (whom I had the privilege of praying with to receive Jesus) into my home office after a small group meeting one night. I showed him how to make a web page and even signed him up for his own web site. This helped establish a fast friendship between us. It catapulted us into a new dimension of sharing. Now, we weren't only talking about "spiritual things" in the small group, but were sharing our interests and hobbies with one another. One small group leader wrote, "A woman in our small group had just undergone back surgery and was recuperating in the hospital. After a call to her, we decided to go and visit her instead of having our regular meeting at home."[7] This group was clear about its priority: community first.

➤ Contact them outside of the small group. I'm referring here to a phone call, a note of appreciation, a cup of coffee together, or a formal visit. Your effort in getting to know the small group member outside the group will pay rich dividends later. You'll build loyalty between you and the person.

Points to Remember

By example, the leader can guide the group to new levels of communication using principles such as restating the idea, dealing with conflict, and offering encouragement. Remember:

➤ Great communication encourages others to participate.

➤ Don't allow certain people to dominate the meeting. Learn how to deal with those who talk too much.

➤ Conflict is normal and natural in a small group. Learn how to deal with it.

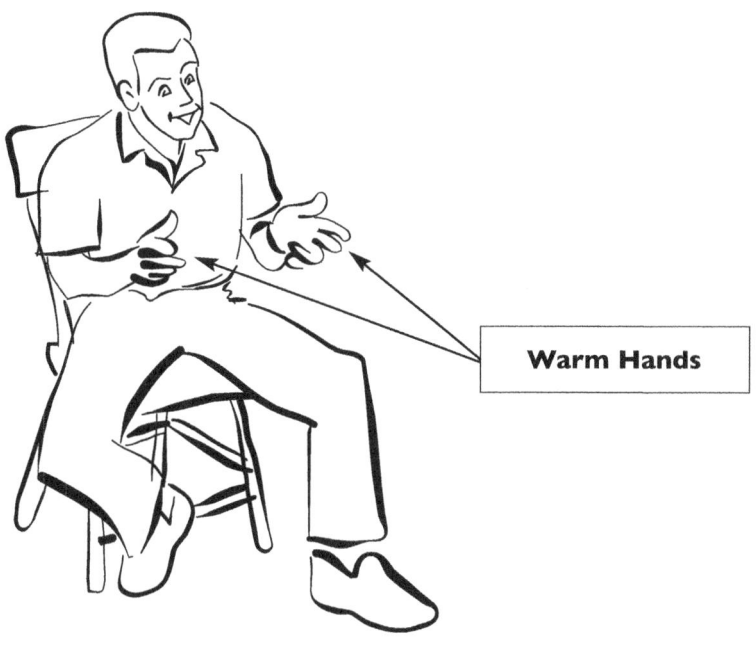

Warm Hands

Warm Hands

Small group leaders need great hands, hands that reach out and point others to Christ. Such hands help small group members reach out together and warmly welcome the hurting and disillusioned into the group.

Chapter Eight

Warm Hands: Reaching Out to Non-Christians

We've often seen pictures of Christ's hands reaching out to a lost and dying world. In reality, those are our hands. He has chosen to use our hands to invite a lost world into relationship with Him.

One of my favorite icebreakers is this: "Who was the most influential person in bringing you to Christ?" You'll hear responses like: My brother, a friend at work, a relative, and a teacher. Only a small percentage will mention a stranger.

The fact is that very few people are brought to Christ by strangers. In reality, those closest to us have influenced us the most. The evidence tells us 70-90 percent follow Christ as a result of relational evangelism. According to the studies, the most natural form of evangelism is the type that takes place through loving, caring relationships.

Poll about Christian Influence[1]

The Institute for American Church Growth conducted a poll among 14,000 people from a variety of churches and denominations, asking them the question "Who or what was responsible for your coming to Christ and the church?" The results:

➤ A special need 1-2%
➤ Walk in 2-3%
➤ Pastor 5-6%
➤ Home visitation 1-2%
➤ Sunday School 4-5%
➤ Evangelistic Crusade . . .0.5%
➤ Church Program 2-3%
➤ Friend or Relative . .75-90%

Few non-Christians wake up one Sunday and decide to attend a church meeting. Those who do receive the *jolt* to attend a church service don't normally stay because they don't have friends in the church.

There are many other examples in the Bible of people influencing their friends, co-workers, and loved ones to Christ. In John 1:35-46, we read about Andrew's relationship to Simon and Philip's relationship to Nathanael. Lydia and the Philippian jailer both led their families to follow Christ (Acts 16:15; 16:31-33). Cornelius brought his fellow soldiers and family members to hear the Gospel (Acts 10:1-2, 22-24). And Matthew introduced his friends and fellow tax collectors to Christ (Matthew 9:10). Relationships are the bridges that the Gospel travels across to touch lives.

An effective small group leader will constantly remind members to become friends with non-Christians and to develop those relationships. One of the best ways to do this is to follow the example of Jesus by meeting a need before discussing spiritual issues.[2]

An Outreach Lifestyle

While staying in the home of Steve and Claudia Irvin[3] I observed:

➤ They hold a weekly English-speaking class for non-Christians in their home (an outreach tool).

➤ One morning, Steve knocked on my bedroom door at 7 A.M., informing me he had plans to play golf with a non-Christian friend. "I hope to win this upper-class businessman to Christ," Steve said. "At this point, he won't darken the door of a church."

➤ While eating breakfast that morning, the doorbell chimed and in stepped a non-Christian housewife from the same apartment complex. After introducing us, Claudia said, "We're going for a walk around the neighborhood. I'll be home later."

➤ The next day, Steve and Claudia had to fly out of the house because they were going to exercise in the local gym. Why? You guessed it — to meet non-Christians.

➤ Two days later, the house was once again filled with non-Christians learning English. On my last day, Steve arrived home late because he was playing basketball with non-Christian friends.

Pastor David Cho writes, "I tell my group leaders, 'Don't tell people about Jesus Christ right away when you meet them. First visit them and become their friend, supply their needs and love them.' Right away the neighbors will feel the Christian love and will say, 'Why are you doing this?' They can answer, 'We belong to Yoido Full Gospel Church, and have our own small group here, and we love you. Why don't you come and attend one of our meetings?'"[4]

Invite Those Whom God has Placed in Your Life

God has placed your home in a strategic place. He's placed you in your particular neighborhood. He's given you particular friends. As you reach out to unbelievers, you'll make an exciting discovery: The Holy Spirit has arrived ahead of you! He's giving them a hunger for Christ and preparing their hearts. As you look for signs of the Holy Spirit working in your friends' lives, also notice the lives of those close to them. Get to know those close to them. Many times a relative or friend of the person you are ministering to is close to responding to Christ. This person may be the key to unlocking the heart of your friend and many others in that network of relationships. Let God open your eyes to how He's working in various lives you are touching.

These natural webs of relationships raise exciting possibilities for outreach.

The small group can provide such friendships. The small group becomes a second family to many. In the small group, these family relationships are often established before the non-Christian attends the church's large weekend service.

Random Acts of Kindness

Alton P. LaBorde Sr. writes: One of the key ways I've met and invited people to small groups is by helping people, strangers, who are in the process of moving. They may have a truck or a trailer loaded with furniture, and I just follow them to their destination and help them unload. On several occasions, I've used my truck and 16-foot-long trailer to assist them.[5]

What is an *Oikos?*

The word *oikos* is found repeatedly in the New Testament, and is usually translated "household." The word refers to one's primary group of friends — those who relate directly to us through family, work, recreation, hobbies, and neighbors.

The Evangelism Cycle

Johnny invited Mary to her university small group. Mary received Christ and Johnny nurtured her to become a faithful disciple of Jesus Christ. Mary's hunger for the Word grew and within months she was leading her own small group, reaching out to her friends who didn't know Jesus Christ. Mary now has her own disciples whom she trains to lead small groups. Five of her close university friends now know Jesus Christ as their personal Savior as a result of her testimony.

Frequently, a non-Christian is hesitant to immediately enter a church building. It's much easier to first participate in a small group in the warmth of a home. Dale Galloway writes, "Many people who will not attend a church because it is too threatening, will come to a home meeting."[6] Later, these same non-Christians will go to church with a friend they've met in the small group.

Although each person's experience is different, research shows that, on average, a person hears the Gospel seven times before responding to it. Keep this in mind. When you share your testimony or invite someone to a small group or church and they don't respond to Christ, realize they might need more time.

The key word is *invite*. Herb Miller sums up the difference between growing churches and non-growing churches in one word: "invite." Miller says, "70 to 90 percent of persons who join any church in America come through the influence of a friend, a relative, or an acquaintance. No amount of theological expression from the pulpit can overcome a lack of invitational expression from the pews."[7]

Identifying a Non-Christian in Your Small Group

One small group used a code to identify whether someone is a non-Christian in the group. If the small group member says to the rest of the group, "I've invited a special friend tonight," then everyone knows that the person is a non-Christian. This signal is especially important for the leader. After knowing the facts, a sensitive small group leader will discern how best to relate to the non-Christian.

Because most people need to hear the Gospel several times, it's important to provide different opportunities for them to hear the message.

Evangelize as a Team

Small group evangelism is a team ministry. Small group leaders who mobilize the group to view evangelism as the first priority maintain small group health. In Mark 1:17, Jesus tells a group of fishermen, "I will make you fishers of men." But fishing alone on the side of a river with a pole in hand definitely was not what Jesus and His fishermen friends had in mind! When they fished they did it as a team using nets. Their fishing involved multiple people and sometimes even multiple boats (John 21:6; Luke 5:6-7). Fishing with a net is far more effective than with a pole. Christ calls us to work together as we gather people to Him.

The tools of the fisherman — the net and the fishing pole — best illustrate small-group evangelism. Small-group evangelism uses the net to catch fish. In every sense of the word, it is group evangelism. Everyone participates.

Larry Stockstill of Bethany World Prayer Center describes it this way: "The old paradigm of 'hook fishing' is being replaced by teams of believers who have entered into partnership *(community)* for the purpose of reaching souls together. . . . Jesus used the "partnership" of net fishing to illustrate the greatest principle of evangelism: our productivity is far greater together than alone."[8]

David Cho, senior pastor of the largest church in the world, said, "Our small group system is a net for our Christians to cast. Instead of a pastor fishing for one fish at a time, organized believers form nets to gather hundreds and thousands of fish. A pastor should never try to fish with a single rod but should organize believers into the 'nets' of a small group system."[9]

Non-Christians can see Christ in your life, but they can see Him even more clearly as you introduce them to other Christians, because they see Him not only in each individual life but also in your relationships with each other.

Many people feel uptight about outreach because they think it means confronting strangers or forcing their views on others. Yet, there are many natural ways to build relationships with non-Christians. Birthday parties are an easy way to include both groups at a fun and

Steps to Reach Out[10]

➤ Each member selects one non-Christian.

➤ Each member commits to initiate contact with that person within the next several weeks for the purpose of building a relationship. (Invite these non-Christians into your life before inviting them to the group.)

➤ During each meeting (during the Works time), members share how the friendship is developing.

➤ The small group diligently prays for these people, as well as for the group members. Pray that God will soften the hearts of the non-Christian friends. Ask Jesus to create opportunities for the building of friendships. Ask God to make it clear when the time is right to invite your friends to your group.

➤ A "harvest event" is scheduled for one month later. The idea is to plan a "neutral" group function (a dinner, a picnic, a women's luncheon, or game night). A one-day retreat or social function that includes a short devotional may be ways to ease your friends into the spiritual aspects of the group.

➤ Members then invite their friends to the harvest event. Make your harvest event seeker-sensitive. Go to great lengths to make everyone feel welcome.

➤ Share the importance of group life by talking about the benefits of the group using personal examples.

➤ Re-invite your friend to the group when the opportunity arises. Through ongoing prayer and follow-up, many invitees continue attending the small group and eventually the worship service.

relaxing event. Other friendship-building activities include holidays, meals, neighborhood parties, and sporting events. Common hobbies and interests are also good ways to bring people together.

Inviting Non-Christians to Special Occasions

What special social events of your small group or church could you invite them to? Are there other Christian events, dramas, or concerts they might enjoy going to with you?

My wife Celyce is great at inviting non-Christians to carefully planned small group events. She uses crafts, holidays, and meals to attract non-Christians. Two neighbors attended her Tuesday small group. Celyce persisted with both of them. They didn't respond immediately, and she had to keep on inviting to finally reap the fruit.

One of them has now received Jesus and is attending our church.

Special events, such as a dinner, picnic, or thematic small group (e.g., one focusing on an issue like marriage, God's existence, etc.) are a great way of reaching non-Christians. I think it's a great idea to rent a video and tie the lessons of the video into the Bible. On one occasion, a group in which I was involved watched 15 minutes of the movie *Schindler's List*,

The Matthew Small Group

The Matthew Small Group is a break in the regular small group cycle wherein full attention is given to the people in our lives who need Christ, or need to follow him more seriously. Setting apart special time to focus on the people in our *oikos* (sphere of influence) is essential to help your small group members persevere with unbelievers in their lives. One important note: though you may have special periodic meetings, such as the Matthew Small Group, that focus on outreach, never forego the weekly "share the vision" time in your group, where you articulate the goal of the group to multiply disciples. We must be encouraged regularly to press on with our relationships.

Creative Ideas for Inviting Non-Christians

➤ Begin with a barbecue. Many people will come to a barbecue before attending a small group.

➤ Have the meeting at the home of the member who plans on inviting a new person. It's much easier for a non-Christian person to enter a "friend's home," rather than attend a meeting in a stranger's home.

➤ Hold an icebreaker night. This might include interactive group games.

➤ Show the JESUS video with the purpose of inviting non-Christians to attend.

➤ View parts of a secular video that lends itself to eternal questions.

➤ Plan a retreat with your small group; go on a group bike ride; invite non-Christian friends to join the fun with you.

➤ Fill your empty chairs. Use some of the ideas above to invite new folks to your group.

➤ Look around on Sunday morning. Invite someone new or someone not in a group yet.

and then prepared questions on the meaning of eternity. On such occasions, you can invite people *because* of the special event taking place.

Transparent Sharing Wins People to Christ

The small group is an exciting place to reach people for Christ. The atmosphere of the home builds caring, warm relationships. In this context, the *facts of the gospel* come through not as cold propositions but as living truths visible in the lives of others. People are naturally drawn to Jesus Christ. Non-Christians can ask questions, share doubts, and talk about their own spiritual journeys. Oftentimes our failure to be honest is probably the greatest hindrance to people receiving Jesus Christ.

Transparent sharing in the small group reveals to non-Christians that believers are indeed not perfect — just forgiven. One of Satan's chief tactics is legalistic deception, trying to convince people that God requires unreachable standards and that only "good" people enter heaven. Small-group evangelism corrects that misconception. Open sharing gives unbelievers a new sense of hope as they realize Christians have weaknesses and struggles too. The difference is that Christians

The Door   *by Sam Shoemaker*

I admire the people who go way in.
   But I wish they would not forget how it was before they got in.
Then they would be able to help the people who have not yet even found the door;
   Or the people who want to run away again from God.
You can go in too deeply, and stay in too long,
   And forget the people outside the door.
As for me, I shall take my accustomed place,
   Near enough to God to hear Him, and know He is there,
But not so far from men as not to hear them,
   And remember they are there, too.
Where? Outside the door - thousands of them, millions of them.
   But - more important for me - one of them, two of them, ten of them. Whose hands I am intended to put on the latch.
   So I shall stay by the door and wait for those who seek it.
"I had rather be a door-keeper ..." So I stay near the door.

place their sin and struggles at the foot of the cross of Jesus.

Jay Firebaugh counsels: "So when an unbeliever shows up in your small group, do everything the same (except pray silently that the Holy Spirit will reveal to the visitor his or her need for Jesus). If you carry on your gathering as usual, with Jesus in the midst of the group, the nonbelievers will witness the reality of a true relationship with Christ."[12]

Christ told his disciples their love would draw the world to Himself. More than just a prayer of unity, Christ's prayer for His disciples in John 17 is a call to evangelism. Jesus says: "My prayer is not for them alone. I pray also for those who will believe in me through their message . . . may they also be in us so that the world may believe that you have sent me" (John 17:20-21). To many, unity and evangelism mix as well as oil and water. They appear to be opposites that repel each other. Christ tells us, however, that unity among believers attracts non-Christians to God.

In Wesley's small groups, everyone was expected to speak freely and plainly about every subject, from their own temptations to building a new house. Within this framework of "open sharing," many were converted. The hearts of sinners melted as they interacted with "saved sinners." Jesus Christ made all the difference.

10 Reasons Not to Reach Out[11]

➤ If people start becoming Christians, we'll need a bigger room to meet in.

➤ Praying for two friends to come to know Jesus isn't in my job description.

➤ If everyone in my small group wants to go to India this summer, I'll have to go too.

➤ Taking risks isn't good for my disposition.

➤ If we become known as Christians in our dorm, people might start asking us questions about our faith.

➤ Revival isn't in my one-year plan.

➤ Serving the poor might make me uncomfortable with my lifestyle.

➤ If our group stays small, everything will be under control.

➤ Telling people about Jesus isn't politically correct.

➤ Trusting God to use our small group to make a difference on campus, in the community, and in the world is too much to ask.

Prayer

The Scripture tells us in 2 Corinthians 4:4 that: "The god of this age has blinded the minds of unbelievers, so that they cannot see the light of the gospel of the glory of Christ, who is the image of God." Only prayer can break the hold of the enemy.

Satan and his demons have blinded people's minds, and they're unable to see the gospel of Christ. Paul also says in Ephesians 6:12: "For our struggle is not against flesh and blood, but against the rulers, against the authorities, against the powers of this dark world and against the spiritual forces of evil in the heavenly realms."

If we're going to see our friends, family, neighbors, and work associates won to Christ, we must pay the price in prayer. Effective small groups and small group leaders are dedicated to prayer. They recognize the most effective tool to win non-Christians to Christ is fervent prayer. They take the words of Paul seriously: "Devote yourselves to prayer, being watchful and thankful" (Colossians 4:2).

Praying for Non-Christians[13]

➤ *The "empty chair" prayer* – Leave one chair empty during each group meeting to represent one or more lost friends. Ask your group members to gather around the chair and pray for the salvation of the lost people in their *oikos* (sphere of influence).

➤ *Prayer partners* – Pair up group members who will pray daily for each other's lost friends. These partners can hold each other accountable.

➤ *Concert prayer for the lost* – Introduce a new kind of prayer to your group! At your next meeting, ask them to stand and pray aloud simultaneously for the salvation of specific lost friends. It can be noisy, but it's a powerful "rumble" of prayer that puts Satan on notice!

➤ *Prayer walking* – Walk in pairs through a targeted community, praying for salvation to come to each home or apartment you walk past. This is a great way to prepare a new host home for your group meetings.

➤ *Create a "Blessing List" Poster* – Use a pre-printed poster or a piece of butcher paper and write the names of lost people on it. Post it on the wall and pray for these people each week, making plans to connect them to the members between meetings.

Points to Remember

The Scripture tells us "God was reconciling the world to himself in Christ, not counting men's sins against them. And he has committed to us the message of reconciliation" (2 Corinthians 5:19). God now uses our hands to introduce a lost, hurting world to Himself. Remember:

How to Pray for Non-Christians

Pray for God:

➤ To give them a hunger for Christ.
➤ To remove all barriers keeping them from responding to Christ.
➤ To bless each area of their lives.
➤ To make Christ real to them.

➤ Effective evangelism cultivates the natural friendships and relationships that God has placed in our lives.
➤ Small group evangelism is team-oriented rather than individual-oriented.
➤ Non-Christians are attracted to special small group events (e.g., small group dinner, video, picnic, etc.).
➤ Transparent sharing within the small group often wins others to Christ.
➤ Prayer is the most effective tool to win non-Christians to Christ.

Walking Together

Walking Together

The journey of a thousand miles begins with a single step. Our feet provide direction to the rest of our body. Knowing which steps to take will help the small group leader chart the journey, knowing that a predictable road lies ahead.

Chapter Nine

Walking Together: Moving Through the Stages of Life

My mother was a college professor in the discipline called child development. When our daughter Sarah was young, we would often call my mom with urgency in our voices, "Is it natural for Sarah to act like this?" "Yes, dear," my mother responded. "In fact, you can expect her to manifest these characteristics." Almost mystically, she would predict Sarah's tendencies for her age period. My mother's advice was founded in the scientifically based patterns of children that age.

As a small group leader, you'll gain confidence by knowing how to walk the group through predictable small group stages. The experts in small group dynamics have analyzed these stages (called by a variety of names), and you can find reams of material on this subject. This chapter will give you a starting point.

Small Group Stages

➤ *Forming Stage:* Focus on icebreakers and social gatherings.

➤ *Storming/Norming Stage:* Focus on honest application of God's Word and prayer.

➤ *Performing Stage:* Focus on reaching out to non-Christians and allowing others in the group to minister.

➤ *Reforming Stage:* Focus on leadership development and reproduction.

Forming Stage

"Is this the type of group I want to get involved with?" Tom asks himself during the first few weeks of Jim's small group. Most of the members in Jim's group are asking the same questions. Roberta Hestenes writes, "When a group first meets, each member tends to experience conflicting feelings of attraction and repulsion. While having chosen to be there, they are still testing the group to see if it can be a satisfying and worthwhile experience for them. Each wonders whether or not he will be accepted."[1]

People really want to know if this group is the right fit for them. A young couple will be seeking like-minded fellowship. Take John and Mary. They're a "yuppie" couple, looking for fellowship with other such couples. Yet, they notice the small group mainly consists of older couples and even a few older single divorcees who talk a lot. Even though John and Mary feel lots of love, they'll have to weigh their options. Will they stay? Or is it better to look for another group? People should not feel compelled to stay in the group.

During this first stage, the group members are looking to the leader for direction and vision. The leader must be transparent and provide non-threatening, group-building relational activities. The leader sets the tone by always telling his or her story first. Self-disclosure continues as the leader allows and encourages each member to tell his or her story, providing positive feedback through affirmation. The leader uses a variety of facilitative devices to help members share their story, thus reducing their anxiety and beginning to build trust.

The group should focus on icebreakers, testimonies, and close social times. The goal during this stage is relationship building, not Bible study, missions, or worship. You might say it's the icebreaker stage.

Forming Stage

➤ *Strategy of Leader:* To clarify purpose, direction and goals. Above all, the leader must model transparency by sharing openly and honestly.

➤ *Activities:* Icebreakers, vision casting and social times (e.g., refreshments, picnics, etc.)

Storming/Norming Stage

Stage two is characterized by shock, patience, and grace. Conflict among group members often occurs during this stage. Conflict is a natural and healthy part of the group-building process (within limits), especially as members become more comfortable with each other and risk sharing their own views.

During this stage, the group members take off the masks and let their real personalities shine through. Doug Whallon writes, "They [group members] know they are accepted and therefore do not need to wear masks . . . because they know they have been forgiven by God."[2] Members are more willing to test out their real opinions in front of the group to see how the others will react. As members share opinions that are contrary to the opinions of others in the group, conflict may occur.

The leader, therefore, must display empathy, understanding, openness, and flexibility. He or she must model ministry while preparing members for greater involvement.

The end of this stage marks the beginning of group ownership. *The* group becomes *our* group. In short, the group is now ready for more serious commitment. Those who are more committed will be your core group.

Performing Stage

During the first two stages, members desire to explore each other's personalities, and communion is a high priority. This emphasis can easily wear thin, if the group doesn't fully enter into the ministry stage. The danger is that group members will

Storming/Norming Stage

> ➤ *Strategy of Leader:* To display empathy, understanding, openness, and flexibility. To model ministry, while preparing members for greater involvement.
> ➤ *Activities:* Dynamic worship, in-depth sharing during lesson time, and fervent prayer.

Confessions of a Small Group Director[3]

"I find that groups don't instinctively and intentionally pursue service outreach projects without a good deal of leadership encouragement from small group coaches and myself. Perhaps it is our natural tendencies that cause groups (and for that matter churches) to become ingrown rather than freely serving others with the love of Christ."

Performing Stage

➤ **Strategy of Leader:** To release others to minister. The leader must spot, train (or make sure potential leaders receive training), and release future leaders. The leader directs the group less during this stage, encouraging others to lead parts of the group (e.g., icebreaker, worship, etc.).

➤ **Activities:** Outreach events, which might include evangelistic dinners, videos, picnics, etc. The Works time is given paramount attention.

Evangelism

"Evangelism is just one beggar telling another beggar where to find bread." — D.T. Niles.

engage in "navel-gazing" and fail to reach out to include new people in the group. When a small group has been together too long, it can become ingrown. Newcomers are viewed as intruders and seldom return.

A group that doesn't reach out tends to die a painful death. Just as Jesus said, ". . . unless a kernel of wheat falls to the ground and dies, it remains only a single seed. But if it dies, it produces many seeds" (John 12:24).

A pastor friend recently took on a new small group assignment in a church. After a few months he wrote, "I am here trying to solve the North American small group riddle. The biggest challenge for groups here in the U.S. is getting evangelistic momentum. If they don't get evangelism working they stagnate and then the pastors give up." New converts make a small group exciting, and the leader should encourage proactive outreach.

In this stage, outreach is the priority. The leader must plan to involve the entire group in various outreach events. The leader must direct the group to pray for non-Christians, plan harvest events, and invite new people to the group.

The leader must also release others to minister, recruit leaders for training and deployment, and challenge others to risk for Jesus. The leader is less directive during this stage, encouraging others to lead parts of the group (the icebreaker, worship, and so forth).

Reforming Stage

Birthing — that is, multiplying —

All Kinds of Ministry Projects

Visit www.kindness.com where there are literally thousands of ideas for service projects. This is a great resource for service ideas.

a new small group can be one of the most exciting events in the group. At the end of the performing stage, the successful group will multiply by sending out designated leaders to form a new group (or groups).

Birthing should be seen as a celebration, not a separation. Remember, the Lord "added to their number daily" (Acts 2:47). The Lord has caused the growth; we must respond by keeping His work going and starting new groups. Like cells in the human body, small groups must multiply or face stagnation.

Giving birth to new groups needs to be a core value. I believe that in the first meeting, the leader should say, "We hope the Lord adds to our group, and our goal is to celebrate the birth of a new group later on as well."

Don't Wait Too Long[4]

One small group pastor counseled a group that has been meeting more than two-years, "...This group should have multiplied long ago. Just as the gestation cycle lasts for nine months, so should the life cycle of the small group. The reason [this leader] can't figure out what stage his group is in is because they should have already experienced all the stages. The water has broken. It's time to P-U-S-H! It's time to go into the world and multiply!"

Groups that multiply must be rewarded, and the leaders should be recognized.

Growing small group-based churches around the world position multiplication as the chief motivation for ministry. It's best to involve the *entire group in the decision process*. If possible, the group itself should be involved with such questions as:

➤ When will the new group begin?
➤ Who will lead the new group?

First Century Birthing[5]

The small group was meeting together for the last time. Their leader was leaving, the members were unreliable. Some in the group were divided and even vying for positions of prominence. One member was exposed as a fraud and thief. Defeat and fear best described that last meeting. Yet, the leader boldly proclaimed, "Don't let your hearts be troubled. Trust in God . . ."

The leader was Jesus, the dysfunctional small group was the twelve disciples, and the meeting happened just hours before Christ was arrested, tried, and executed.

Reforming Stage

➤ *Strategy of Leader:* To make final preparations for a new leader to guide the daughter group. The leader must allow the new facilitator to guide the entire small group in preparation for leading his own group.

➤ *Activities:* The leader talks to the group frequently about the importance of new birth. Fervent prayer is offered in the Works time for the new small group. Hold a celebration party (frequently called a "birthday party") in the parent group right before the birth of the daughter group.

➤ Who (members) will leave the existing group to become the core members of the new group?

Some small group researchers promote terminating the group after one year. I advise you to think in terms of multiplication rather than termination. Small groups are born to multiply, rather than die.

Never allow the small group stages to hinder the multiplication of your small group. I've heard this excuse before: "I can't multiply my group because we haven't experienced all the stages." Wrong! You can multiply your small group whenever you have a trained leader — whether or not you've passed through all the group stages.

You don't have to have a certain number of people attending your group before multiplying. You should multiply the group whenever you

Time it Takes to Multiply a Small Group

➤ Multiplication depends on receptivity levels. Small groups multiply more rapidly in places like Brazil, Latin America, and Africa. In other places, like Europe, multiplication takes longer.

➤ In some cases (e.g., groups that started with all non-Christians), it's wise to change leadership, switch members around, or anything else that can kick-start the group to multiply.

have a trained leader. This leader might take one to three people from the original group to form the new group.

Small group stages are like an X-ray machine. They are designed to help you see the normal process of a group. But just as the X-ray machine can't cause your body to grow, small group stages will never initiate growth and new birth. To do this, you'll need to start training new leaders from the very beginning of your small group.

Empty Nesters

On several occasions, my wife and I have felt like "empty nesters" after we've multiplied our Thursday night small group. We longed for the former members, but we realized we needed to begin again. The knowledge of small group cycles helped guide us to the next step.

You Can Multiply Without Completing Each Stage

➤ These stages will give you a general guideline of most small groups. However, small groups are always open to receive visitors. With the inclusion of new members, the cycles might start and stop along the way.

➤ It's wise to multiply when you have trained leaders, rather than waiting for a certain number of people in your group.

**Top Ten Lame Excuses for not
Multiplying (Birthing) the Group**[6]

➤ We're looking for quality, not quantity.
➤ Why would we want new group input?
➤ "Multiply?! Since we've started to reach out to the schizophrenics at the hospital, I feel like we multiply every week!"
➤ There won't be "seconds" on Sandra's cherry cheesecake!
➤ Doesn't that leave stretch marks?
➤ I might have to give up my cushy recliner for a cold steel folding chair.
➤ We don't need to; we only have about 20 people coming to our group.
➤ Visitors, Shmisitors!
➤ My children are too young to explain the "Birthing Process."
➤ Birthing is just not my gift.

This is my prayer for you as you work your way through each stage in your present group. Knowing these stages and applying the leadership principles for each one will fine tune your leadership and give you more confidence to hang tough for the long ride.

Points to Remember

The knowledge of small group stages will help walk your group through the natural progression of small group life. Remember:

➤ Small groups *normally* pass through four stages.
➤ The initial *forming* stage is a time to get to know members of the group.
➤ The *storming* stage is characterized by conflict as the members form deeper relationships.
➤ During the *performing* stage, the solidified group is better prepared to reach out to others.
➤ The *reforming* stage is a time to give birth to another group and start the process over again.

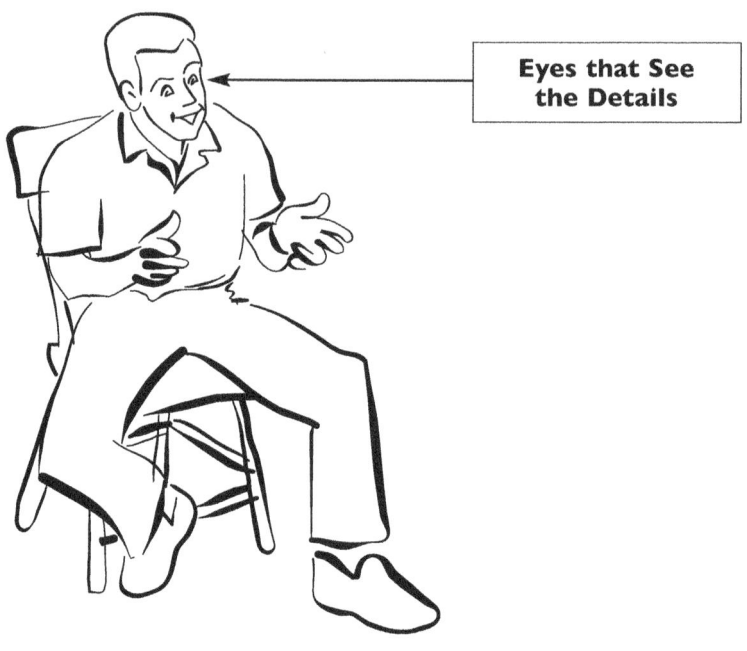

Eyes that See the Details

Eyes that See the Details

Small group leaders with 20-20 vision see the smaller details (refreshments, temperature, etc.) as well as the larger issues (the lesson, multiplication, etc.). To really see the details requires thoughtful reflection before and after the meeting.

Chapter Ten

Eyes that See the Details

I once heard a professor share some wise counsel with a group of preachers: "On Sunday morning, *before* you ascend to the holy pulpit to preach God's inerrant Word before a waiting, hungry congregation, *take a moment to make sure that your pants' zipper isn't down.*" He knew the main point would be missed if the details were left undone.

Take a moment to view the details. The eyes of effective leaders glance around the room to make sure the song sheets are distributed, the phone is off the hook, and the chairs are arranged in a circle.

Details matter. They matter to God and they matter to your people. Imagine the incredible detail of the Old Testament temple. God asked Moses to follow His plan precisely, down to the smallest details.

Atmosphere of Home

We grow accustomed to the smells in our homes, but visitors sense them immediately. Pets, things children spill in odd places, heavy perfumes, the evening dinner, and even room deodorizers can irritate visitors. You know all about your home. You may even like its smell. But others might not be so enthusiastic. Think about their noses.

If you have young kids, be sure to dispose of the dirty diapers before the meeting starts or take the hamper of laundry to the washing room. God wants us to be one in Christ, but don't purposely test the oneness of your members by allowing strange smells to flood the room!

Make sure to clean the guest bathroom before the small group begins. Is there toilet paper, soap, and a clean hand towel?

Temperature

The temperature in the home increases as more people are packed into a room. Members can become agitated and uncomfortable for the lack of fresh, cool air. If your people must wear heavy coats in your house, although you're in the heat of summer, you probably need to adjust the temperature. The main thing is that you're sensitive to the needs of those in the room. One expert advised that 67 degrees is an ideal temperature for home groups.[1] Common sense is probably a better temperature gauge.

Seating Arrangement

Arrange the seating so each person can see every other person in the group. A circle is the best choice.

"Top Ten Reasons to Stop Meeting at Your Host's Home"[2]

➤ When it gets so comfortable that he doesn't bother to put a shirt on for the meeting.

➤ They have new white carpet and pick up every crumb that falls with one hand while carrying around vacuum cleaner in the other.

➤ The host's idea of an icebreaker is their vacation videos.

➤ You're tired of finding cat hair in your coffee mug.

➤ The fellowship times double as a "painting party."

➤ They thought indoor plumbing was just a fad and would never catch on.

➤ For the past few weeks there has been a sign on the host's door, "come on in and please turn on the coffee pot," ...but they never show up!

➤ The cats outnumber the group members 10:1.

➤ The host's home is so near the nuclear reactor that when you turn the lights off the hosts glow in the dark.

➤ The host charges for parking!

As the leader, place your chair so it's on the same level as the rest of those in the group — neither at the focal point nor in the background.

If your house is spacious, it's best to move the chairs into a close circle, thus occupying only a portion of the room.

Just remember that large rooms may be excellent for large groups, but they kill discussion in small groups. When people are spread far apart (as is the case in large houses), it's harder to openly share thoughts and feelings.

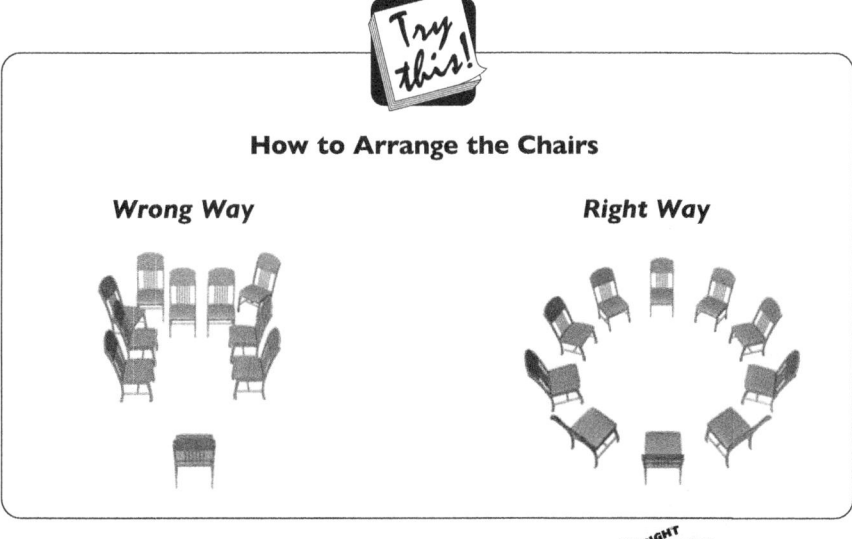

How to Arrange the Chairs

Wrong Way   *Right Way*

Some people feel intimidated about opening their homes because they're not as large or luxurious as those of other group members. Don't listen to this argument.[3] Actually, a small apartment or home generates closeness and reminds the group that, at eight to twelve people, it's time to prepare for a new group.

Lighting

The lighting should be bright enough for everyone to read but low enough to feel cozy. If it's too dark,

Keeping it Small in Mexico City

In this city of 25 million people, houses and apartments are extremely small. Room size means limiting the maximum size to ten people. Ten is an ideal size. The tiny living rooms constantly remind the group they need to give birth to daughter groups.

people will have a harder time following the worship sheets and other handouts. You may feel this is unimportant, but details do matter. It's the little things that often make the difference.

Materials

Provide materials for everyone. They'll thank you for it. I've been in small groups where there were only a few song sheets. I shared a song sheet with the person next to me, whom I didn't know. I found myself concentrating more on holding the music steady than on worshipping Jesus. Spend the extra money and make sure everyone has his or her own copy.

I never handed out lessons to each member. I simply invite them to follow along in their Bibles and then ask them relevant questions that apply to the text of Scripture (though having extra Bibles on hand is a good idea).

No Five-Course Meals

Don't allow refreshments to become a burden — or worse yet, a point of competition. If you have trouble financially and need help with refreshments, by all means ask other members of the group to contribute.

When David Cho first started small groups in his church, he noticed competition among members to top last week's refreshment time. Finally, Pastor Cho had to make it a rule to only provide a simple, non-costly dessert.

Refreshments

Refreshment time isn't something tacked on to small group ministry. It's a vital part of it. The refreshment time is often the best moment to ask personal questions, enter deeper communion, or even reap the harvest.

I mentioned earlier that some groups provide chips and dip during the icebreaker time *and* after the final prayer. If you can financially afford both, great. If you have to choose, serve refreshments afterwards.

After the meeting, we sometimes serve the people while they're still seated. Most of the time, we stand around the dining room table. This gives the most freedom for people to move around, talk freely, and visit individually. On rare occasions, we'll sit down as a group at the dining room table.

Eating refreshments normally lasts about 15 minutes. Afterwards, people will drift out at their own pace.

It's the small group leader who sets the tone. If the small group leader is open to it, the people may stay for more than an hour. If the small group leader needs a cut off time, the people will know it.

Personally, I think that one hour of talking and sharing is sufficient. Our group *normally* spends one-half hour in fellowship after the small group. My group starts at 7:30 P.M. and ends at 9 P.M., and the people normally leave about 9:30 P.M. (there are exceptions, of course, to any rule). Depending on your personality, you may desire more or less time afterwards.

Maximum Communion

Some groups always sit together at a table for the refreshment time. This maximizes group communion. On the negative side, it's harder to develop individual relationships in this atmosphere (e.g., follow-up, personal questions, etc.), and some might need to leave immediately after the meeting. Variety is the best rule here.

Sensitive leaders take advantage of this time to make personal contacts, greet visitors, and reconfirm previous decisions. Be proactive during this time. Don't wait until people come to you. Go to them.

Children in the Small Group

I hesitate even talking about this as a *detail* of small group ministry. In truth, whole books are written on children's small groups, and I wrote one of them: C*hildren in Cell Group Ministry.*[4] But since this book is focused on adult leadership, I'll include only a few simple observations:

The ages of the children make a world of difference. If children are six or under, they'll need more activities, such as singing, games, visual aids, or videos. This age group will obviously not benefit as much from an adult group. For this reason, some groups choose the option of providing reasonably priced childcare (some churches even provide free child care during the meeting time).

My preference is for children to begin experiencing group life at a young age. Here are a few suggestions on how to make it work:

Children: More than a Detail

One of the largest churches in the world is the Elim Church in San Salvador, El Salvador. Over 110,000 people attend the small groups each week. Half of those are children.

Ten Worst Childcare Options[5]

➤ "Baby bungee jumping"
➤ Hanging them from hooks by the front door.
➤ Give the kids cans of spray paint and let 'em go!
➤ Play hide-and-seek in the church basement, but go find them an hour later.
➤ Veggie Tales!
➤ "We have a dog that is great with kids!"
➤ A Simpson's Marathon.
➤ Tell them if they can stand in the back of the church and pray for an hour, you'll buy them a Wii.
➤ Send them to the basement with a 12-pack of Surge.
➤ Tell the sitter, "Sure, you can invite your boyfriend's rock band over."

➤ Allow the children to stay in the adult group for the icebreaker and worship time. During the Word time, the children can leave the adults and receive a personalized Bible lesson directed by one of the members (if necessary, the members can rotate in teaching this time).

➤ When the group has four or more children, pray that God will provide an adult or teenager who desires to lead a children's small group. This might be someone from your own adult small group or from your church. The children can then meet with their small group leader (s) in a different room of the same house for the entire meeting (or at least for the lesson part). This is a normal, permanent children's small group that promotes a similar order — icebreaker, worship, lesson, prayer, and outreach. The church should provide material for the children's small group leader and all the support necessary.

➤ Another option is to hold small groups for children in various neighborhoods around the city. Adults would lead these small groups. These afternoon groups are a lot like the small groups of *Child Evangelism Fellowship*

Children Need Discipleship

Daphne Kirk says, "The children in your group need discipleship for the same reasons as the adult! Each child is a unique, profoundly precious individual in the eyes of God and their parents. For that individuality to be recognized early in life, they need someone who knows where they are in their relationship with Jesus and the problems they face."[6]

Distractions

Guard against distractions. Turn off cell phones ringers and place the pets in another room or outside. Turn off TV sets, radios, and computers during a meeting. Yes, our lives are busy all the time, but during the one and a half hours of the small group, you should focus on the group 100 percent. Don't answer the phone.

My wife and I have made a deal to let the phone ring even if it's a member saying he or she will arrive late. Does it really matter if the group has already started? Just concentrate on those present.[7]

Child Evangelism Fellowship and Good News Clubs

Good News Clubs meet in the neighborhood where children live. Boys and girls ages 5 through 12 gather with their friends to sing songs, memorize God's Word, and apply God's Word to their lives. At each group gathering, an opportunity to receive Jesus Christ as Savior is given.

What about when your own children — who are supposed to be sleeping — start crying during the small group? Make sure you and your wife have a strategy for taking care of them. Which of you will leave in the middle of the lesson when one of them starts crying? Just make sure one of you is assigned to the task.

Time to Start

A common frustration among small group leaders is getting groups started on time. It's not unusual to wait five or ten minutes past the

Checklist to Avoid Distractions

➤ Are cell phones on vibrate or mute?
➤ Is the temperature approximately 67 degrees?
➤ Are the seats arranged in a circle?
➤ Are there enough seats?
➤ Is there sufficient light in the room?
➤ Are there enough song sheets? Bibles?
➤ Are the refreshments ready?

scheduled starting time while waiting for members to arrive.

The leader must make a decision. Will the group start on time or wait for the last few members to arrive? Two simple steps can help leaders conquer this age-old problem.[8]

Agree on expectations. Ask the group what they think about starting on time. This is the ideal time for the group to establish clear expectations and the importance (or unimportance) of group members arriving on time. Most likely, the group members will agree that arriving on time is important. The most critical element is agreement among group members. Remember also that you can continually review this commitment when new people are added.

Begin on time. Perhaps it seems obvious that the leader should start the group on time when battling chronic lateness. However, as mentioned earlier, many leaders don't start on time because they're waiting for all the participants to arrive. Delaying the beginning of group time sends several mixed signals to group members:

➤ "This meeting really doesn't start at 6:30; it starts at 6:45."
➤ "It's OK if I arrive late; they won't start without me anyway."
➤ "The first 15 minutes of the meeting isn't important."

If a small group leader begins on time regardless of latecomers, he or she is sending the signal that every part of the meeting is important. The leader is also making wise use of the limited time that's available for the meeting. Ultimately, if a small group leader is in the habit of starting on time, people will arrive on time. Conversely, if a leader does not start on time, the members will arrive later and later.

Time to Close

I don't believe that a small group meeting should last longer than one and a half hours. I like to say to leaders: *If you don't strike oil in one and a half hours, stop boring.* David Cho, senior pastor of the Yoido Full Gospel Church, recommends that a meeting last no longer than one hour.

Small group members have a host of responsibilities, which include going to work, spending time with family, and numerous chores. A member might think twice about attending the next week if the meeting is too long.

Dealing with the Latecomers

Even if you have a clear starting time, you may still have individuals who chronically arrive late. This calls for frankness between the leader and the chronically late group member.

God's Blessing on Your Home

With all these details, you might feel hesitant about hosting a small group. Before saying no, consider God's blessing upon your home.

When someone opens his home for a small group, the Spirit of God is invited to reign in that house. God will certainly honor your step of faith and abundantly bless your house and all that you have. He did with Obed.

In 2 Samuel 6:10-12, we read how God blessed the house of Obed-Edom because of the presence of the ark of the God:

> He [David] was not willing to take the ark of the LORD to be with him in the City of David. Instead, he took it aside to the house of Obed-Edom the Gittite. The ark of the LORD remained in the house of Obed-Edom the Gittite for three months, and the LORD blessed him and his entire household. Now King David was told, "The LORD has blessed the household of Obed-Edom and everything he has, because of the ark of God." So David went down and brought up the ark of God from the house of Obed-Edom to the City of David with rejoicing.

Formally End the Meeting on Time

Stand, hold hands in a circle, and lead in a prayer of conclusion at the stated ending time — even if you're in the middle of something! Don't wear out your welcome, especially among those who have children and need the time to prepare for the next day. The weekly gathering is only one small part of group life. The balance must be lived out in homes and relationships all week long!

Opening your home for a small group doesn't require God to bless your home. Yet, through the worship, prayers, and study of Scripture, you'll be inviting the living God to bless you and your home.

Points to Remember

Small group leaders with 20-20 vision see the distractions before they become stumbling blocks. While concentrating on the larger issues, they don't neglect the details. Remember:

➤ The home atmosphere plays an important role in attracting and maintaining members.
➤ Arrange the seating in a circle.
➤ Make sure there's sufficient light in the room.
➤ Provide song sheets for everyone in the group.
➤ Children are an essential part of the small group and must receive ministry.
➤ Prevent distractions by preparing for them.
➤ Start on time and close on time.

Chapter Eleven

Keep Learning and Growing

The best leaders never stop learning. You could call them lifetime learners because they realize there's always more to learn. They grow as they go. John Kotter, professor at Harvard Business School, says, "Lifelong learners actively solicit opinion and ideas from others. They don't make the assumption that they know it all or that most other people have little to contribute. Just the opposite, they believe . . . they can learn from anyone under almost any circumstance."[1]

Frank is a lifetime learner. The first time he led a small group, he talked too much, failed to listen, nervously shifted from question to question, and finished late. He would have received a "2" on a scale of 1-10 (for effort alone). Yet Frank refused to throw in the towel. He committed himself to work on his listening skills, to use open-ended questions, and to facilitate. He learned to wait in silence after asking a question, allowing others the time to formulate their responses. He improved to the point that he could even deftly handle a talkative member of the group.

The most important trait in Frank was his commitment to abide in Christ. He dedicated himself to spend daily time in Christ's presence, receiving personal strength and insight for his group.

Frank is now scoring an "8." He hasn't arrived but he's improved greatly.

Follow Frank's example and keep learning. Don't give up. God desires to develop you into a great small group leader.

Notes

Introduction

[1] Robert Wuthnow, *I Come Away Stronger: How Small Groups Are Shaping American Religion* (Grand Rapids, MI: Eerdman's Publishing Company, 1994), 45. Robert Wuthnow's ground-breaking survey of small groups in the U.S. not only discovered that 40 percent of the U.S. adult population is involved in a small group, but that 7 percent who were not currently in a small group planned on joining one within the following year.

[2] Lyle E. Schaller, *The New Reformation: Tomorrow Arrived Yesterday,* (Nashville, TN: Abingdon Press, 1995), 14.

[3] The Elim Church in San Salvador has 110,000 people attending the 11,000 small groups. The International Charismatic Mission has an equal number in their 20,000 small groups and now rent the local indoor stadium each weekend (47,000 people attending the four services). Similar statistics exist in Dion Robert's small group-driven church in Ivory Coast, West Africa. Faith Community Baptist Church in Singapore and Bethany World Prayer Center in Baker, Louisiana are also prime examples of the growth of the small group-driven church worldwide.

[4] John K. Brilhart, *Effective Group Discussion*, 4th Edition (Dubuque, Iowa: Wm.C. Brown Company Publishers, 1982).

[5] As small group size increases there is a direct decrease of equally distributed participation. In other words, the difference in the percentage of remarks between the most active person and the least active person becomes greater and greater as the group's size increases [John K. Brilhart, *Effective Group Discussion*, 4th ed. (Dubuque, Iowa: Wm. C. Brown Company Publishers, 1982), 59].

[6] The general headings in this section were taken from Michael Mack's, "What a Small Group is Not," *Small Group Dynamics* (Internet newsletter of the Small Group Network, November, 1999).

[7] I'm referring to the Love Alive Church in Tegucigalpa, Honduras. For a long time, this church waited until the group had fifteen people before multiplication. Experience has taught them, however, that it is difficult for a group to maintain an average of fifteen people over a long period of time. As a result, the leadership changed the number to ten. Now when a group has an average of ten people attending on a regular basis, it is a prime candidate for multiplication. Dixie Rosales, the Small Group Director, told me that the change from fifteen to ten members helped revolutionize small group multiplication in the church. Now, many more groups qualify for multiplication and the proliferation of groups is spreading more rapidly throughout the whole church.

[8] Carl George, *How To Break Growth Barriers* (Grand Rapids, MI: Baker Book House, 1993), 136.

[9] John Mallison, *Growing Christians in Small Groups* (London: Scripture Union, 1989), 25.

[10] Dale Galloway, *The Small Group Book* (Grand Rapids, MI: Fleming H. Revell, 1995), 145.

Notes

Chapter 1
[1] Stephen Covey, *The 7 Habits of Highly Effective People* (New York: Simon & Schuster, 1989), 151.

Chapter 2
[1] TOUCH® Publications sells a book dedicated entirely to icebreakers (call 1-800-735-5865 or go to www.touchusa.org) NavPress sells an excellent book called *101 Best Small Group Ideas* (Colorado Springs, CO: NavPress Publishing Group, 1996; www.navpress.com. The *Serendipity Bible for Groups* is loaded with excellent icebreaker questions: www.serendipityhouse.com/pages/home.html.
[2] These points were taken from an article by Dan Smith and Steven Reames entitled, "Leading Worship in Small Groups," *Small Group Dynamics* (Small Group Network, September 1999).
[3] Tami Rudkin, "Worship Works," (Small Group Network, April 2000).
[4] Jay Firebaugh, *Cell Church Magazine*, Spring 1999, 15.
[5] Judy Johnson, *Good Things Come in Small Groups*, (Downers Grove, IL: InterVarsity Press, 1985), 176.

Chapter 3
[1] This small group took place in Liberia, West Africa during a short term mission trip in 1982.
[2] Robert Wuthnow, *Sharing the Journey* (New York: The Free Press, 1994), 267.
[3] Admittedly, not all small groups focus on participation as I'm promoting in this book. The leaders at Yoido Full Gospel Church, the Elim Church, and the International Charismatic Mission teach the lesson. They do not see themselves as facilitators as much as preachers and teachers. I would not equate these groups as "Bible studies" because these groups focus on non-Christians just as much as believers. Small groups in other churches do promote participation. Ralph Neighbour, for example, has done more than anyone I know to promote member participation in groups. The small groups at Faith Community Baptist Church in Singapore (the church that Ralph Neighbour helped establish) are 100 percent participatory. Even before I absorbed the small group-driven church philosophy, I wholeheartedly promoted group participation and the small group leader as a facilitator rather than a Bible teacher.

Chapter 4
[1] David Hocking, *The Seven Laws of Christian Leadership* (Ventura, CA: Regal Books, 1991), 63.
[2] *The Leadership Challenge: How to Keep Getting Extraordinary Things Done in Organizations* (Jossey-Bass Publishers: San Francisco, CA, 1995), 167.
[3] Ralph Neighbour Jr., "Questions and Answers," *Cell Church Magazine*, Vol 2., No. 4, 1993, 2.
[4] *The Art of Mentoring: Lead, Follow, and Get Out of the Way* (Houston, TX: Bullion Books, 1998), 46.
[5] Howard Snyder, *The Radical Wesley & Patterns for Church Renewal* (Downers Grove, IL: InterVarsity Press, 1980), 55.
[6] Howard Snyder, *The Problem of Wineskins, Church Structure in a Technological Age* (Downers Grove, IL: InterVarsity Press, 1975), 89.
[7] Judy Hamlin, *The Small Group Leader's Training Course* (Colorado Springs, CO: NavPress, 1990), 54-57.

Chapter 5
[1] Taken from Michael Mack's article "What's Questionable about These Questions", *Small Group Dynamics*, (Small Group Network, February 1996), and Deena Davis, compiler, *Discipleship Journal's 101 Best Small-Group Ideas* (Colorado Springs, CO: 1996), 19.
[2] Jim Egli, *Cell Church Magazine*, Spring, 1999.
[3] Christian A. Schwarz, *Natural Church Growth* (Carol Stream, IL: ChurchSmart Resources, 1996) quoted in Larry Kreider, "Obstacles to Growth," *Cell Church Magazine* Vol. 6. No. 4. Fall, 1997, 22.
[4] For more information on caring for leaders, check out *How to be a Great Cell Group Coach,* published by CCS Pubishing.

Chapter 6
[1] Stephen Covey, *The 7 Habits of Highly Effective People* (New York: Simon and Schuster, 1989), 239.
[2] Michael Mack, "Kinesics," *Small Group Dynamics* (Small Group Network. [n.d.]).
[3] Judy Hamlin, *The Small Group Leader's Training Course* (Colorado Springs, CO: NavPress, 1990), 51-80.
[4] Michael Mack, "Kinesics."
[5] I taught a small group seminar in Cambodia and one of my sessions was on transitioning to the small group-driven church model. In my PowerPoint® presentation, I had many examples of offices and church buildings. What I didn't take into account was the fact that Cambodia was desolated because of the war and couldn't relate to my examples of church buildings. Because of my lack of preparation and careful thought, I used illustrations that were culturally insensitive. The comments on the evaluations made this very clear to me!
[6] Tom Peters, *Thriving on Chaos* (New York: Harper Perennial, 1987), 176.
[7] Stephen Covey, *The 7 Habits of Highly Effective People* (New York: Simon and Schuster, 1989), 244.
[8] Ralph Neighbour, "Jesus is the Real Cell Leader," *Small Group Dynamics* (Small Group Network, January 2000).
[9] Remember that some personality types require that the leader ask a person to respond by name. This is especially true of the High S (Steady) on the DISC personality profile, so if you sense that Sue is ready to share, call upon her.
[10] Roberta Hestenes, *Using the Bible in Groups* (Philadelphia: The Westminster Press, 1983), 29.
[11] Viktor Frankl, "Youth in Search of Meaning," *Moral Development Foundations*, (Donald M. Joy, ed., Nashville: Abingdon, 1983), as quoted in John C. Maxwell, *Developing the Leader Within You*, (Nashville, TN: Thomas Nelson Publishing, 1993), 118.
[12] Author unknown. Poem that I wrote down while studying at Prairie Bible School in Three Hills, Alberta Canada. I used this poem in several sermons, but never wrote down the reference.

Chapter 7
[1] Richard Price and Pat Springle, *Rapha's Handbook for Group Leaders* (Houston, TX: Rapha Publishing, 1991), 116, 117.
[2] I encourage you to use the other methods first before trying this technique. If the above techniques fail to silence the talker, this one will lay out clear ground rules and will give you a solid ground to approach him or her in the future if the rule is violated.

Notes

[3] Adapted from Pat J. Sikora, "Dealing with Conflict among Members," *Small Group Bible Studies: How to Lead Them*. Logged in on Friday, February 25, 2000.

[4] Henry, Matthew, *Matthew Henry's Commentary on the Bible*, (Peabody, MA: Hendrickson Publishers) 1997.

[5] B.A. Fisher & D.G. Ellis, *Small Group Decision Making: Communication and the Group Process*, 3rd ed. (New York: McGraw-Hill, 1990), 264 as quoted in Julie A. Gorman, *Community that is Christian: A Handbook on Small Groups* (Wheaton, IL: Victor Books, 1993), 195.

[6] Barbara J. Fleischer, *Facilitating for Growth* (Collegeville, MN: The Liturgical Press, 1993), 84.

[7] *Cell Church Magazine*, Summer, 1996, 11.

Chapter 8

[1] Wayne McDill's *Making Friends for Christ* (Nashville, TN: Broadman Press, 1979), 28 and Jim Egli in *Circle of Love*.

[2] In John 5 Jesus heals a paralytic (verse 8) and only later calls him to repentance (verse 14). In chapter 8 Jesus stands up for the woman caught in adultery (verse 7) and subsequently extends forgiveness to her and challenges her to change her lifestyle (verse 11). In John 9 Christ heals a man who had been born blind (verse 7) and sometime later invites the man to a personal faith in Him (verse 35). These people opened up to Christ after He had shown them practical love and let God display His power. In the same way, our witness to different people will begin in different ways. Like Jesus we should start at their point of need and continue from there to show and tell them of our Savior.

[3] Missionaries with the Christian and Missionary Alliance in Bogota, Colombia.

[4] Peggy Kannaday, ed. *Church Growth and the Home Cell System* (Seoul, Korea: Church Growth International, 1995), 19.

[5] *Cell Church Magazine*, Summer, 1999, 13.

[6] Dale Galloway, *20-20 Vision*, (Portland, OR: Scott Publishing, 1986) 144.

[7] Herb Miller, *How to Build a Magnetic Church*, Creative Leadership Series. Lyle Schaller, ed., (Nashville, TN: Abingdon Press, 1987), 72-73.

[8] Larry Stockstill, Notes from the Post-Denominational Seminar, May, 1996.

[9] Cho quoted in Karen Hurston, *Growing the World's Largest Church* (Springfield, MI: Chrism, 1994,) 107.

[10] I derived the basic steps from Janet Firebaugh's article, "Fishing Together," *Small Group Dynamics* (Small Group Network, October 1999).

[11] Jimmy Long, Anny Beyerlein, Sara Keiper, Patty Pell, Nina Thiel and Doug Whalon, *Small Groups Leader's Handbook* (Downer's Grove, IL: InterVarsity Press, 1995), 87.

[12] Jay Firebaugh, *Cell Church Magazine*, Summer 1999, 11.

[13] Karen Hurston, "Preparing for Outreach through Evangelism-Based Prayer," (Small Group Network, July 2000).

Chapter 9

[1] Roberta Hestenes, *Using the Bible in Groups* (Philadelphia: The Westminster Press, 1983), 32.

[2] Doug Whallon, "Sharing Leadership," in *Good Things Come in Small Groups* (Downers Grove, IL: InterVarsity Press 1985), 65.

[3] Dan Lentz, (Small Group Network, July 2000).

[4] Small Group Network, April 2000.

[5] Dan Smith, "Multiplication," (Small Group Network, 1996).

[6] Taken from "Top Ten Lame Excuses for not Multiplying (Birthing) the Group," *Small Group Dynamics* (Small Group Network, September 1999).

Chapter 10

[1] Michael Mack, "Top 10 Ways to Facilitate so Your Group Can Participate" *Cell Church Magazine* Vol. 8, no. 2 (Spring 1999), 22-25. I'm grateful to Michael Mack's article for providing the ideas behind the sub-headings used in this chapter. I also included some of his material from that excellent article.

[2] Small Group Network, April 2000.

[3] I don't buy the argument that says you need to have an expensive home to open a small group. If you live in a lower-class area, most likely the majority of the homes will be like yours. Neighbors will be glad to attend. Even with homogeneous groups, it's likely that you'll invite "your kind of people" (people of your social status, background, etc.).

[4] The most complete guide on children in small groups is *Feed My Lambs* by Lorna Jenkins (Singapore: Touch Ministries International, 1995).

[5] Small Group Network, July 2000.

[6] Daphne Kirk, "Are Your Children being Discipled," *Cell Group Journal*, Winter 2000, 12.

[7] Once I was consulting with a small group of Christian leaders. The wife kept on jumping up and answering the telephone. I felt like my advice wasn't very important — like her next phone call was far more important. Now project this to your group members. They won't feel important if you're prioritizing the telephone, your computer, or your dog over them.

[8] The principles behind this list were taken from an article by Mark Whelchel entitled "Chronic Lateness," *Small Group Dynamics* (Small Group Network, June 1999).

Chapter 11

[1] John Kotter, *Leading Change* (Boston, MA: Harvard Business School Press, 1996), 182.